a most formidable union

the history of DATA and TASS

a most formidable union

the history of DATA and TASS

researched and written by
tony foley

foreword by
ken gill

MSF

london 1992

A Most Formidable Union
The History of DATA and TASS

Published by MSF
Park House, 64/66 Wandsworth Common North Side, London SW18 2SH

Design, typesetting and page make-up by Trask Pinchuck Partnership
Drummond House, 203 North Gower Street, London NW1 2NL

Printed by Spider Web, London

Front cover photo: Lockout protest at the Teeside shipbuilders

British Library Cataloguing in Publication Data

ISBN 0 946 553 99 8

contents

foreword

Tony Foley's History of DATA and TASS is an important contribution to the story of British trade unionism. It is written with humour and some panache, as well as being detailed and analytical. Some may not agree with all its judgments on events or individuals but almost everyone will enjoy the style.

This history is in one sense incomplete. While it refers to the Transfer of Engagements made by craft unions to TASS in the early 1980s, it does not go into details or into the history of the various craft sectors. This is because this book is essentially about the recent history of white collar trade unionism in the engineering industry. In other words it is a history of the staff union TASS and how it developed out of the AESD and DATA. The craft and manual unions which came to TASS in chronological order were the National Union of Gold and Silver Allied Trades (NUGSAT), the National Union of Sheetmetal Workers Coppersmiths Heating and Domestic Engineers (NUSMWCH&D), the Association of Patternmakers and Allied Craftsmen (APAC), the National Society of Metal Mechanics (NSMM) and the Tobacco Workers. These were all long established unions each with a rich history of its own.

Most trade union history is seamless such that it is sometimes difficult to see the joins. It is important to know the background of AESD, a rather elitist craft union for draughtsmen, and to understand that the formation of DATA represented a break from this tradition, although most members would not have necessarily recognised it as such. DATA, of course, prepared members for their new life within the AEUW and the potential this represented. Unfortunately, as Tony shows, this potential was never realised. This was due, I believe, to a mixture of historical antagonism between manual and non-manual workers, and political sectarianism.

Ken Gill

Most activists saw that the potential of craft unionism "a la AESD" had been exhausted by the early 1960s. In this decade of trade union growth it became possible to organise a much broader spread of white collar workers into unions in all sectors of the economy. This was best achieved by existing organisations with deep roots in the industries concerned, even if some activists resented losing their exclusive craft image. But it was several bridges too far to suggest that white collar trade unionism could simply be subsumed into the mainstream of manual organisation. This was never understood by the leadership of the AEU, left or right, and is why the

AUEW project eventually failed. For while craft attitudes and organisations had reached the end of their separate possibilities, white collar workers required autonomous structures which reflected discrete interests and different levels of trade union consciousness. Only if these facts were recognised would it have been possible to build the AUEW as an all skills, all occupations industrial union.

Once the AUEW project was perceived to be "dead in the water" the TASS leadership turned its attention to the alternatives. It is then that TASS saw itself as the centre for a manufacturing based union bringing in a number of craft unions while preserving industrial autonomy and democratic structures. Initially there was the possibility of reviving the AUEW project. But once this was no longer feasible the link with ASTMS to form MSF became the best way forward. Thus a white collar engineering technicians union reached out to become part of a general but generally skilled union as comprehensive in industries and sectors as the Transport and General Workers Union, but with its future joined with advancing technologies.

Ken Gill

how the union got its name

Shipbuilding and engineering draughtsmen at John Brown's Shipyard on Clydebank in 1913 discovered that white collar staff did not enjoy a special relationship with the employer. Largely due to rumours of war, the order books of engineering companies were filling up. Experienced draughtsmen and designers were in demand. Those who had the qualifications believed they would be in a position to sell their skills to the highest bidder. What they failed to appreciate was that capitalist market mechanisms were never intended to benefit labour.

In cahoots with other firms in the industry John Brown's management decided on a tactic which would effectively neutralise labour market forces. The employers agreed among each other that they would not offer pay increases to induce draughtsmen to leave one firm and join another.

Once the draughtsmen saw what the employers were up to they were furious. For the first time many of them came face to face with a fundamental fact of industrial life, the inherent conflict between employers' and employees' interests. The outcome was that the affronted draughtsmen hired a hall in Glasgow, called a meeting and unanimously agreed that the situation would require collective action. They decided to form a trade union.

How they went about it and how they succeeded in developing arguably one of the most efficient white collar unions in the manufacturing sector has been told in J E Mortimer's definitive "History of the Association of Engineering and Shipbuilding Draughtsmen".

Draughtsmen approach a problem by planning exactly what is required and considering how it will function. They then break everything down to constituent parts, detail these and finally produce a general assembly. There is something in their psyche which tells them that if you can envisage it in your mind, you can draw it and if you can draw it, you can make it.

This kind of thinking led to the creation of a trade union for a group of skilled, white-collar workers who up until this time did not believe they would need one.The aim of the pioneering members was to construct a tightly knit organisation which would become an efficient negotiating machine. To back up its administration they devised a uniquely successful communications network which linked drawing offices, locally, regionally and nationally. By the middle of the century the draughtsmen and tracers had built a 50,000 strong association and had made an emphatic impact in the engineering industry and in the wider trade union movement.

Trade unions express in institutional forms the reaction of working people to the growing complexity of production technology. The division and multiplication of industrial processes compelled wage earners to form collectives as a defence against exploitation. The titles they gave their unions, associations and societies either defined their membership in precise terms or indicated that they had an industry-wide operation.

Draughtsmen thought in exact terms, they were nothing if not accurate. The title "Association of Engineering and Shipbuilding Draughtsmen" declared exactly what one had to do for a living and where one had to do it in order to qualify for membership.

Traditionally, the career of a draughtsman went via a shopfloor apprenticeship in one of the skilled engineering trades, a course in technical education, usually part-time and, eventually, a position as a junior draughtsman. Versatility, ingenuity and a certain artistic flair, tempered with shopfloor practicality, were characteristics which were more likely to be found in drawing offices than in other white collar areas. It was these qualities which enhanced their perceived role in the engineering industry. Draughtsmen were not inclined to undervalue their contribution to industrial output. They had substantial reasons for believing they were entitled to worthwhile salaries and favourable conditions of employment. These beliefs stimulated and motivated the successful advance of the union.

Arising from the demands of World War II, draughtsmen played a significant part in advancing production technology. Whether they were aware of it or not, many of the innovations which they had helped to devise were diminishing the range of functions which were normally carried out in the drawing office. A new breed of white collar technician was appearing, with new job titles such as Progress and Methods Engineer, Work Study Engineer, Technician Assistant, Expediter and even "Job Chaser". The question now was who was going to organise and represent members of staff who worked in close relationship with the drawing office but who were, apparently not qualified to join the AESD.

Active members had been pondering this issue. Their deliberations surfaced at the 1943 Annual Conference. In moving a resolution from the Paisley Branch Mr W Gillan said that if the Association were to recruit the categories of technician it should change its name. Mr W Kenyon from London South-West went a step further and proposed an amendment to the Paisley Motion. The title, he said, should be the Draughtsmen's and Allied Technicians' Association. The amendment and the original motion were narrowly defeated. There the matter rested.

Technology did not rest. New and more efficient methods of production continued to be developed. Job titles under the heading "technician" were multiplying and many of the new posts were being filled by draughtsmen for whom they represented a step up the promotional ladder. The AESD Rule Book declared that the Association provided organisation for draughtsmen, designers, calculators, estimators, planning engineers and tracers. But in spite of this, active members in many companies were in some confusion about whom they could, or could not, recruit. Persuading people to join the union was one thing, gaining recognition to negotiate for them was another. Engineering employers always pretended to be shocked at the idea of a Draughtsmen's Association representing people who did not actually work at a drawing board. Nor was the situation made any easier when other white collar unions were beginning to pick up the limboed technical staff and establishing a presence in what was once an AESD fief. The Association of Engineering and Shipbuilding Draughtsmen was becoming less significant in the technical staff sectors of industry.

After an interval of twelve years from the time the matter was last officially raised, the 1955 Annual Conference accepted a motion from Hatfield Branch which said the name of the union ought to be changed. The following year the EC presented a Report to Conference confirming that a change of name was desirable.

The first Rule in the Rule Book identified the Association by its full name. There was a three-year interval between meetings of the Representative Council (Annual Conference) at which revisions to Rules could be dealt with. A successful alteration to Rule required a majority of two-thirds of the delegates. 1957 was the next available year in which a motion changing the name could be introduced. Consequently, the delegates at the 1956 Conference instructed the Executive Committee to bring in the following year an enabling motion which could give effect to the change.

Came 1957 and the Executive Committee presented a motion saying the name of the union should be "The Draughtsmen's and Allied Technicians' Association". Prior to the Conference a "water testing" circular to the branches indicating the proposed name change had shown a majority in favour. The EC was confident that its Motion was going to win the day. It did. It was approved by the majority of the delegates, but it failed to get the two-thirds it needed to become effective. As draughtsmen were wont to say "Back to the drawing board". Another three years would have to pass before Conference delegates would get the opportunity of considering again a change of name.

The disappointed supporters of the EC's Motion had come to the conclusion that the message was not getting across. At the 1958 Conference they proposed that a sub-committee of delegates should be elected to prepare a report on the changes which were taking place in industry and how these were affecting draughtsmen. The President, however, gave an undertaking that if the idea of a sub-committee was withdrawn he would ensure that the EC would have such a Report ready for presentation at next year's meeting. This was agreed. The Report was produced and put to the 1959 Conference. It stressed that a change of title was absolutely vital and that the EC must have permission to bring forward in 1960 yet another enabling motion to allow the appropriate Rule change to be made. Permission was granted.

It was quite evident that the general feeling among the members was in favour of a change of title for the Association. But the issue was not without its bones of contention. A small articulate minority still maintained that the Association of Engineering and Shipbuilding Draughtsmen should stick to the name its founders gave it. There was also a clear split in the ranks of those who wanted a change. Some believed that the Association should now come right out and call itself a "union", others were equally committed to the retention of "association".

The 1960 Annual Conference of the Representative Council was destined to become the symposium where draughtsmen, whether from the traditionalist or from the progressive camp, were to demonstrate their obsession with terminological exactitude.

Mr E G Elliott, presiding, called for the mover of Motion No.2 on the Agenda, from Coventry East Branch. Mr S M Wilcox stepped to the rostrum.

Motion No.2 said "this Representative Council agrees that the name of the Association of Engineering and Shipbuilding Draughtsmen be changed to the "Draughtsmen's and Allied Technicians' Association".

Mr Wilcox argued that the time had now come when the name must be changed to embrace the whole of the technical workers within the drawing office and the subsequent departments which followed on from the drawing office. He pointed out the problems which arose in trying to recruit technical staff who were not draughtsmen into a draughtsmen's association. The new name would be shortened to 'DATA': "something which was concise, something which, as technical workers, they were referring to day by day and year by year".

The delegate from Belfast South, Mr T Montague, seconded the Motion and also indicated how appropriate DATA was for a union which wanted all technical staff within its ranks.

With the Motion moved and seconded the President called for the first amendment. It came from the Executive Committee and was moved by one of its most influential members, Mr G Fowler. The amendment said "The title of the Association be altered to "The Union of Draughtsmen and Allied Technicians".

Mr Fowler took the delegates through the history of the name change issue. He went back to 1955 and showed that the necessity to change the name was now obvious to the majority of members. The previous year Conference had accepted the EC's Report on the changes in industry which were making the position of the AESD untenable and had asked it to bring forward an enabling motion.

This amendment was intended to meet that instruction. It was the EC's view that as the first Rule of the Association stated:'The Society is a Trade Union'. It was, therefore, opportune now to include the word "Union" in the title. The EC amendment was formally seconded. After the President had dealt with a few points of order the debate on the EC amendment got under way.

The first speaker was J Lunney from Northern Ireland, himself a member of the Executive Committee but who was speaking as an individual member of Conference. Mr Lunney launched into an attack on the EC for daring to remove the word "Association" from the title and for going back on its own proposal made at the last Rules Revision Conference which only failed to get a two-thirds majority. He described the EC as circus performers, tightrope walkers, acrobats who turned somersaults. Obviously pleased with this metaphor he threw his punchline, "the EC had decided to turn a half-somersault on a slippery pole and change Association to Union". He hoped the delegates would reject this amendment.

The debate which followed allowed four speakers in favour of introducing the word "union" and four in favour of retaining the word "association". Two speakers wanted no change at all. The delegates then made it evident they had heard all they wanted and began calling for the vote to be taken. Mr Fowler exercised his right to reply even though he believed there was nothing to reply to. He simply pointed out that the majority wanted a name change and he dismissed as nonsense the idea that people would only join a union if it were disguised as an association. The vote was taken and the EC amendment was defeated.

The delegates were now faced with the task of dealing with nine more amendments. These mainly consisted of a series of different combinations of the words "draughtsmen", "allied", "technicians", "engineering", "union", "association" along with a few definite and indefinite articles.

One after another the supporters of each of the amendments trooped to the rostrum. All of them drew heavily on their knowledge of semantics and nuance to assemble the appropriate words into the form of a new title for the Association. But the assembly was unimpressed. One after another the amendments were summarily disposed of. In the end all that was left was the unamended Coventry East Branch Motion.

The debate on what was not a substantive Motion produced its share of predictable rhetoric. Spades were properly designated as such. A full time official took the opportunity to remind the delegates, as if this were necessary, about Datas, an industrious character from Greek mythology who went around collating information to help him win arguments, hence the word data. This was, according to the learned official "the Association's real image". It was inevitable that someone would delve finger deep into Shakespeare and produce "what's in a name". The wind was blowing in favour of the Motion. The ripple of dissent from the few who still insisted there should be no change at all barely registered.

When a card vote was taken it showed 35,265 for the Motion and 14,477 against. The approval of two-thirds of the representative vote had been achieved. The organisation's supreme policy-making body had spoken. The decision to change the name of the Association of Engineering and Shipbuilding Draughtsmen to The Draughtsmen's and Allied Technicians' Association had finally been taken. And nobody remembered that that was what Mr Kenyon from London South-West had proposed back in 1943.

It now seemed that all the Association had to do was order new stationery, new badges and set about recruiting all those new technicians. It came as a shock to the Executive Committee when it learned from the Registrar of Friendly Societies, whose approval is necessary if a registered union should wish to change its name, that a Delegate Conference decision did not meet the statutory requirements. To register a change of name, a union must have the consent of not less than two-thirds of the total members. Members, according to the statute, was everyone accepted into membership who has not been lapsed or excluded. The Branch block voting system did not meet this condition.

Faced with this situation the EC decided to organise a petition to be signed by every member who approved of the name change. Instead of being the first year in the life of DATA, 1960/61 was the year of the AESD petition.

Using its efficient communications system, petition forms were circulated to cover the total membership. "The Draughtsmen" and the "Vacancy List", the regular union publications, were used to explain and to exhort members to sign the petition and allow the decision taken by the delegates at the Representative Council to be carried out. The lists began to trickle back to Head Office and by the time the 1961 Conference came around the requisite number of signatures had almost, but not quite, been achieved.

It came as no surprise when, at the Conference, the anti-change minority saw this technical hitch as an opportunity to have another try at preventing the alteration to the union's name. Mr Tivey, representing Derby No.1 Branch, stated that he was always opposed to the change of title but had accepted last year's EC statement that to do so only required a decision of the Conference. The EC ought to have known what the law required. Mr Tivey complained that in the face of the Association's publications posing the question in bold print "Have you signed the petition?" he was made to feel like a criminal because he hadn't.

But Mr Mogg of Bristol No.1 Branch was having none of it. He deplored the attitude of Mr Tivey who, he claimed, was trying to defeat a democratic decision taken quite properly by the Association's Annual Conference and was, apparently, encouraging other members not to sign the petition. "It was up to each and every member to do all in their power to see that the petition was signed by the greatest possible number of members".

Mr G Fowler, speaking on behalf of the Executive Committee explained that there was never any question of the members being misled. The EC had been aware of statutory requirements for altering the title of the Association. Unfortunately, the advice it received in relation to these was ambiguous. In the end the EC decided that the petition would be the best means of ensuring that the wishes of the delegates expressed at the Annual Conference could be carried out. The delegates accepted Mr Fowler's report.

By the end of May 1961 the petition had attracted over 49,000 signatures, well in excess of the minimum number required. On 6 June, with the approval of the Chief Registrar of Friendly Societies, the union became the Draughtsmen's and Allied Technicians' Association. On 1 August the new title came into general use. The whole process had taken seven years.

Despite the ponderous procedures and diffuse arguments which preceded the renaming of the Association it seemed the ordinary members took it all in their stride. Once it was announced that the official title was DATA, draughtsmen and designers began to submit proposals for a new badge. At first sketches trickled into the monthly journal. Then the trickle became a flood.

Eventually, the Editor, virtually swamped under a deluge of artistic, ingenious, cynical and often humorous variations of the now familiar acronym had to plead "no more please". It must be assumed that during this outpouring of craft skills there was a measurable fall in the production of working drawings from drawing offices all over the country.

When the new badge did become available it turned out to be the old AESD badge with the letters DATA substituted. Perhaps this was a signal to the rank and file that irrespective of all the soul searching nothing too radical was going to happen.

Under the skilful editorship of J E Mortimer the Journal had strongly advocated the need for the Association to address itself to the changes which were taking place in industrial production techniques which would necessitate a new identity. Notwithstanding this forward-looking line the Journal retained its original title "The Draughtsman" for four years after the union had become DATA. The first "DATA Journal" was issued in January 1965.

members identify with DATA

It takes some time for members of a trade union which was formed to represent the interests of a single occupation to adjust to an extension of their industrial perspective. They become used to the services and policies that have been developed through experience in familiar fields. They believe they can, indeed must, rely on their own resources when it comes to dealing with their employer. Conventional wisdom lingers even when the conditions which fostered it are withering away. As J E Mortimer observed in his History of the AESD: "The craft pride of draughtsmen has been an important factor in the success of the AESD and helps to explain why draughtsmen have a good track record in fighting for their own interests".

Draughtsmen were unpredictable in their support of wider trade union and political issues. Consistently they rejected right wing attempts to exclude communists from holding office in trade unions. In the thirties they indicated wholehearted support for the Republican cause in the Spanish Civil War. But they seemed to avoid becoming involved in other unions' strikes. Nevertheless, within the corps of leading activists was an effective presence of progressively- minded members who were aware of the political and industrial restrictions imposed on a narrowly based trade union. The positive response by the membership to the petition for the approval of the new title was the result of good communications and enthusiastic canvassing by active members. But no one would have claimed that it showed a deep commitment among the rank and file to the full implications of the new status.

Less than half of the Association's members contributed to its political fund. There was no single reason why this was so. Some members were opposed to the union's affiliation to the Labour Party, some believed unions should not be involved in politics at all and there were those who took the "contracting out" option to reduce their subscriptions rate (a penny a week was the political contribution in 1960). There was nothing to indicate that the membership behaved any differently from the national electorate. Support for one party or another followed the perceived ebb and flow of the political tide.

What gave the AESD and subsequently DATA its unique character in relation to other white collar unions was the ability to gather together differing strands of political and industrial philosophy and weave them into an effective bargaining organisation.

Convincing draughtsmen that their employers grossly undervalued their craft skills was not a hard job. The union backed claims for better pay and conditions of employment and found ready response in most engineering drawing offices. The Association boldly declared that direct negotiations between an organised workforce and the employer or the employers' collective was the best way to resolve their conflicting interests. Official opinion was that there was no need for any intervention in this procedure by a third party, including the Government. Not surprisingly this was a policy which some critics interpreted as support for capitalist free market economies. But in the councils of the TUC, the Labour Party and the Confederation of Shipbuilding and Engineering Unions, and the many other groups to which it was affiliated, Association delegates argued for clear socialist aspirations - a planned economy and the nationalisation of the key industrial, financial and social institutions. A union's task, it was claimed, was to extract from capitalism the optimum benefits for its members and support the movement which aimed to redistribute the wealth created by industry for the good of all.

Members, particularly those in well-organised firms, found no difficulty in getting behind the Association in its defence of free collective bargaining. They probably believed its left-wing position in the political area was less significant. It was a case of putting up with the politics as long as the union supported them in pressing the boss for more money. It would be difficult to assess how many members either recognised or acknowledged any relationship between vigorous trade union action in the workplace and the underlying political conflict between capital and labour.

Yet as early in its history as 1918 the AESD nailed its political colours to the mast. That very year George Thomson, the Editor of the union's Journal "The Draughtsman" wrote trenchantly:

"Perhaps all our readers will not see eye to eye with us in our visualisation of the industrial outlook as one of struggle between employers and employees. One man is trying to buy a commodity called labour cheaply and another whose monopoly it is, is trying to extract the maximum price for it. That is the naked fact however we may endeavour to gloss over and refine it".

He concluded:

"This recognition of a tacit state of war is the Association's very raison d'etre. It is justified as a fighting machine and when it ceases so to regard itself it may as well cease to exist".

It would be understandable if this chest-thumping declaration from a fledging white collar union with just over 10,000 members were greeted with some scepticism. But this was 1918. The shop stewards' movement was gaining momentum. The reaction of the Government was to set up a committee under Mr J H Whitely MP, to make recommendations that would take the heat out of industrial relations. Whitely's Report called for the establishment of works committees and joint industrial councils and for wage regulation. These proposals were intended to propagate the idea that employers and employees had common interests. In reality the aim was to neutralise union bargaining power.

In the context of the period, George Thompson had made an apposite statement for any union that wished to maintain credibility. The AESD may have dithered a little when the Whitely recommendations were first published but the Executive Committee soon came to the conclusion that Thompson had made a realistic assessment of what trade unionism was about.

Whether the Association was capable of behaving like a fighting machine was not the question; where it would stand when it came to representing the needs of its members, was. That early declamation determined the Association's industrial relations policies for the future. It was in April 1919 that the AESD had its first official strike. But from then on more and more groups of members were prepared to take action if negotiating procedures failed to resolve their grievances. By the time the AESD became DATA there was behind it a trail of hard-won, some very successful, and, indeed, a fair share of disastrous strikes.

The level of militancy generated in the draughtsmen's union was, undoubtedly, affected by the official policy on strike pay.

The nature of drawing office work was in the main to do with future projects and contracts which were a fair distance down the pipeline. A strike by these workers had little or no effect on immediate company output. Many weeks or sometimes months had to pass before the non-availability of working drawings hit the point of production. So, in order to maintain the members on strike for as long as it would take to bring the employer back to the negotiating table, the Association guaranteed strike pay equivalent to what each member took home in a normal week. Strikes at this rate were expensive, but the employers discovered they could not easily force draughtsmen back through economic pressure and that they might be able to hold out long enough to make their absence felt. Recognition of this fact often encouraged employers to reach negotiated settlements. Certain trade union purists looked askance at workers who would only take strike action if they got full pay. They believed there was virtue in workers suffering hardship and making sacrifices to advance their cause. "Paid militants" was the taunt from certain shopfloor workers who themselves had the power to bring all production to a halt by simply downing tools. Not everybody understood the logic of the Association's strike-pay policy. In spite of the occasional jibe, draughtsmen on strike were more often than not helped by the trade unionists on the shopfloor.

Becoming DATA and opening its ranks to other technical staff would result in the Association having a wider sphere of influence. Job functions in areas of primary production could now be covered. It was obvious that the conditions which justified the 100 per cent strike pay were going to change. A review of what was a fundamental AESD premise was on the cards.

Entering the sixties with a membership of around 60,000 and with a new field of recruitment potential opening for the future it was obvious that many of the traditional procedures and dispositions would have to be revised. At the 1960 Annual Conference, held in Llandudno, the name changing Motion from Coventry East Branch said that what it was proposing was "a matter of urgency in the real interest of future recruitment". Yet this exhortation did not result in the draughtsmen delegates throwing caution to the wind. A future Rule change regarding eligibility for membership was amended to define the categories who could join the Association as draughtsmen, designers, calculators, estimators, planning engineers or other technicians whose function is related to design. The Rule continued to require the applicant to be over 25 for full membership and to have at least eight years experience in the engineering and shipbuilding industry of which at least three were spent as a draughtsman, calculator, etc. etc. This was the kind of semantic reshuffle the delegates did not mind. The Amendment was accepted without debate.

It was a different story when at the same Conference the Executive Committee, responding to a Motion passed the previous year, presented a Report with recommendations for a more efficient method of forwarding subscriptions to Head Office.

The traditional method of dealing with members' subscriptions was, to say the least, fastidious.

Elected corresponding members, who were also expected to carry out the "white-collar-equivalent" duties of a shop steward, collected the subscriptions, entered the names and the amounts on a form and sent this to the Branch Secretary. The Branch Secretary would check and transfer each corresponding member's Returns to the Branch Register. A receipt would be produced and the amounts entered on another form and passed to the Branch Treasurer. The Treasurer recorded the details in a ledger, produced a monthly statement, signed it and then had it countersigned by the Secretary and Branch Chairman and, finally, the cash was sent to Head Office. Head Office had, of course, to await the completion of the Annual Audit before it could officially acknowledge the state of the Branch finances.

The above routine in the studied opinion of the Executive Committee had become extremely cumbersome, inefficient and was leading to a loss of members. The procedure being proposed would simply involve the corresponding members forwarding the contributions direct to Head Office where a newly established automated accounting department would handle the recording, receipting and the return of the information regarding arrears, transfers of members, changes in categories, etc, to the Branch Secretary.

In the light of a growing and more diffuse membership it seemed logical that a less amateur means of dealing with routine financial administration was long overdue. But logic does not fare too well against emotion and sentiment. In the draughtsmen's union there was plenty of both.

The Association Vice-President, Mr E Mackenzie put the proposed changes to Conference. He explained the problems being caused by the existing procedure. He detailed the advantages and the economies which would arise from the Executive's proposals. He produced facts and figures to show that the Association would benefit from a clearly more up-to-date method of administrating its finances. He also underestimated the conservatism and the puritanical fervour with which so many delegates would defend the tedious bureaucracy of the traditional branch practices.

In a debate which took up the greater part of a whole day there were seven amendments to the EC proposals and altogether 89 speakers from the floor. But even with an intervention from the very persuasive General Secretary, Mr George Doughty, Conference failed to give the new scheme the two-thirds majority required for its introduction.

In Blackpool in 1962 the Executive Committee put before the Annual Conference a Motion repeating its deep concern at the operation of the subscription routine. Once again it presented the same proposals which it had failed to get implemented in 1960. The General Secretary outlined the problems which were getting worse and appealed for the two-thirds majority needed to bring in the new procedures.

This time the Motion attracted six amendments. Two were defeated, two fell for want of seconders, one was withdrawn and one was remitted. The Motion was carried. Centralised financial administration, afterwards acknowledged as one of the Association's strong features, was at last established. The resistance by active members had been overcome. The ordinary rank and file members were either pleased with the simpler routine or not bothered anyway.

One of the peculiarities of the draughtsmen who took an active interest in their organisation was the demand that it would be in the forefront in support for radical political and social causes while at the same time viewing with suspicion any radical alteration in its own structure.

Nevertheless, other changes could and would take place. What was needed was the assurance that any alteration of custom and practice would have to be properly designed, checked and approved. This meant that the leadership always had to prepare its case carefully before making innovative suggestions. Reform of inappropriate practices would not happen overnight and sometimes failure to respond quickly would result in lost opportunities.

The long delay in reaching a conclusion about the title of the organisation was to some extent due to the time spent on specious argument over whether it should be called a Union or an Association. Evidently it never occurred to those involved that there was any need to give second thoughts to the use of the words "Allied Technicians". There were no reservations about the implied allocation of status in this designation. The strength of the organised draughtsmen came from their belief that they were an elite in the engineering industry. Their history showed they had refused to be put off by the industrial, political and economic hazards which lay in the way towards the establishment of a body to be reckoned with. It was always a part of their make-up to persist in causes which they were convinced were right. Their weakness was never fully accepting that the technology which many of them were helping to develop would one day re-order industrial hierarchies.

It was not surprising, therefore, that even after setting their sails for a deeper excursion into the engineering industry the preoccupation of the majority of members was with the level of draughtsmen's minimum rates. It was somewhat ironic that the union formed to counter the employers' attempts to impose a standard maximum rate of pay for all draughtsmen should concentrate on trying to impose on employers a standard minimum rate below which none of its members were advised to work.

It was in 1923 that the AESD launched what was to become its major campaigning strategy. The idea was to set target salaries for draughtsmen and then to encourage and support them in efforts to get them applied. One of the advantages of being a single occupation union was that it enabled a price to be put on the basic skills it was assumed every member possessed. This would become the minimum rate. It would be up to the members to claim extra payment for work of a higher grade. The target figures were always carefully assessed so that they would be attractive to the majority of the members and at the same time within the bounds of possibility. Comprehensive statistical evidence and detailed economic research provided members with strong cases to argue with their employers. The 100 per cent strike pay ensured there were very few inhibitions over the withdrawal of labour if negotiations broke down.

The minimum rate campaign was a big factor in the AESD's growth from the late thirties to the sixties (allowing for the periodic stop in the national "stop- go" economic pattern). It was also a key factor in the polarisation of the political forces in the ranks of the active members.

Although there were no indications that the engineering employers were in the least interested in having a national agreement on pay scales the debate in the Association was over whether there should be an approach made to negotiate one. One side held that the membership should be encouraged to step up the action at the plants and compel the employers to parley for peace.

problems of growth

The fifties saw the tempo of AESD-backed disputes begin to rise. Claims for higher wages, a campaign for three weeks' holiday and the inevitable victimisation and recognition issues were among the items keeping office representatives, lay and full-time officials and company personnel officers at full stretch. Strikes involving large numbers of members at John Brown Land Boilers Ltd, Clydebank, D Napier & Sons Ltd, Liverpool, Sanders Roe Ltd, North Wales, Oldnam Ltd, Ashton and Centrax Ltd, Devon were just samples of the widespread activity which was taking place during this period. Each month virtually every copy of the union journal "The Draughtsman" carried photographs of Crombie-coated members with expertly designed picket posters formally posing at the gates of some factory of other. No other white collar, and very few shopfloor unions, could match the level of militancy displayed by the AESD. Over the ten years of increasing activity on all these fronts the membership rose from 45,000 to 60,000. By the 1970's DATA had a membership of over 100,000.

Expansion did not come cheaply. By the time the Association had become DATA the cost of industrial action was beginning to cause concern. It was not a question of easing up on the employers and quietly putting to one side the policies that had been determined and confirmed at Annual Conference. Where claims for improved pay and conditions could not be settled through negotiating procedures then the members would be encouraged to take industrial action and, if necessary, go out on strike. Not only that, the Executive Committee, confirming its commitment to trade union solidarity, was urging members to come out with shopfloor workers on stoppages called by the Confederation of Engineering and Shipbuilding Unions. The problem for DATA was to maintain its militant policies and make sure it had the funds to support the members carrying them out. In the year 1959-60 the disbursement of strike pay amounted to around £50,000. In 1960-61 this rose to £91,000 and in 1961- 62 to £139,000. In its Report to the 1962 Annual Conference the Executive Committee made the following statement:

"The Executive Committee draws the attention of the Representative Council to the extremely high cost involved in maintaining the established policies of Conference in regard to providing full financial support to members involved in official strikes in support of the Association's policies.

The Executive Committee believes that Conference must note this position, balancing, on one hand, the advantages which such a policy has brought to the Association and, on the other hand, the extremely high cost in which disputes can involve the Association, particularly when they affect their many members for such a long period of time as has been the case in the dispute at the General Electric Company. This policy can only be maintained as long as the Association has sufficient finance at its disposal to maintain that policy".

They were referring here to a strike of 400 members from GEC's Witton Works in Birmingham and the supporting action of another 40 at the company's offices in Hemel Hempstead. Coincidental with this there were protracted strikes at Clayton Dewandre, Lincoln, at S Carburettor Co Ltd also in Birmingham and at Hopkinson's Ltd, Huddersfield.

The Executive was now advising careful examination of each case and the weighing up of risk and cost against the advantages to be gained. In other words, no adventurousness and the strict observance of agreed procedures. It was not a panic measure, merely one of caution. After all, there was still over a million pounds in the Association's General Fund. However, 100 per cent strike pay was a factor which limited the number of strikes that could be carried on at the one time. One of the consequences was the formation of a queue of groups waiting their turn to get out on the picket lines.

Not unexpectedly this was a situation which led to the occasional manifestation of frustration in those firms where the members had worked up a head of steam and were then told to cool it until a strike taking place somewhere else was settled. Yet, in spite of this, it was a matter of pride that DATA never had an unofficial strike. The only thing unofficial which the EC knew about but never acknowledged was a publication produced by an active member from Nottingham entitled "A Guide to Strike Organisation".

The renewed pages contained advice on how to get maximum effect from industrial action. It gave advice on the setting up of a strike committee, on picketing, propaganda, relations with other unions, relations with the media and techniques for ensuring morale stayed high.

DATA's militant policies were not going to subside under the weight of a financial burden. At the 1970 Annual Conference the General Treasurer, R Whitely was able to boast to delegates that since 1951 the union had paid out over £2 million in strike pay, far and way above the amounts paid by any other union in the country.

However much it endeavoured to demonstrate it was an Association for all technical staff in the engineering industry and however anxious the Executive Committee was to support members who took action to substantiate that image, the structure and thrust of DATA was in the interests of traditional members and those who were covered by the procedure agreement.

Almost 90 per cent of officially backed strikes were in support of claims targeted on minimum wage. In the years 1962-63 strikes lasting three months or more were commonplace. Wage claims at Aveling Barford of Grantham and at Integral Ltd of Wolverhampton went on for thirty and twenty-six weeks respectively. At Eastern Coachworks, Lowestoft the members had to remain on strike for twelve weeks to gain an increase in pay and improvement in holiday entitlement. 120 members at Singers Manufacturing Co, Clydebank had a month long strike to bring the hours of methods engineers in line with those of procedure recognised members. About 100 altruistic members employed by Mirrlees International, Stockport did demonstrate that money was not everything when they remained on strike for 13 weeks to get the Chairman of the Office Committee reinstated after the management had conveniently made him redundant.

In October 1962 the Executive Committee

found it had to introduce a levy of a maximum of one shilling (five pence) on a weekly subscription of two shillings and three pence (eleven pence) to meet the demands for strike pay and the alarming jump in claims for unemployment benefit from £6,500 in 1961 to £40,000 in 1962. Those who were more than twelve months in membership were entitled to £5 per week if they lost their jobs, a clear indication of more problems on the horizon.

It took a lockout in 1967 of all 1,600 DATA members in the Shipbuilding Industry to compel the Executive to reduce strike benefit to 80 per cent of take-home pay. A further reduction to 60 per cent was agreed in 1971 just as the Association was entering the Amalgamated Union of Engineering Workers. Significantly, the intention behind these reductions was to allow more members to be supported in disputes rather than to put the damper on them.

Unquestionably, minimum rates was the single issue which had concentrated the minds of DATA members on the need for keeping a tight operation. At virtually every Annual Conference of the Representative Council there would be a major debate on minimum rates. Often these would resemble a dutch auction as delegate after delegate came to the rostrum to declaim the pay levels below which they would prefer not to work. The Executive Committee, on the other hand, made it crystal clear that whatever rates were agreed at Conference their implementation in a National Agreement would be the result of pressure in the localities. In the plants where the organisation was strong and the office committees gave effective leadership that pressure brought about a negotiated settlement or a strike. There were also the more inhibited groups who would keep their heads down and hope that when a national agreement on improved minimum rates was reached it would be applied to them. DATA could accommodate both types. The strong helped the weak and tolerated the timid. Because of its policy on pay DATA earned for itself the reputation of being "the most formidable white collar union" (The Times).

Throughout the sixties DATA was establishing a significant presence in a list of companies which read like an engineering industry's Who's Who. A random sample would include such household names as: GEC, Rolls Royce, The Metal Box Co, The Dunlop Co, Phillips Industries, Massey Ferguson, Babcock & Wilcox, Standard Telephone and Cables, British Insulated Callender Cables, Lucas CAV. There were important agreements in the motor car industry, for example with Fords, Vauxhall (General Motors), Chrysler UK Ltd, Rootes Ltd, Jaguar Cars and British Leyland. In the aircraft industry DATA played a leading role in representing staff at famous companies such as The British Aviation Corporation, The Westland Aircraft Co, Hawker Siddley, Bristol Siddley Engines and Short Brothers and Harlands. In a few of these firms the procedural arrangements were shared with other white collar unions, mainly the clerical workers CAWU, the Managerial Staff Association ASTMS, and the clerical section of the Transport and General Workers Union ACTSS.

In the public sector, for example Civil Air Transport, the National Coal Board and the gas industry, DATA got its foot in the door through organising their drawing offices and as a result has representatives on Joint Industrial Councils and Industry Advisory Panels. By 1970, after years of dogged persistence and hard negotiating DATA managed to become one of the most important staff organisations in the British Steel Corporation.

Minimum rates was a winning ploy. But for the progress of DATA into the white collar technician jobs it was a handicap. How much could be seen from the employers' response to claims for recognition.

The first national negotiating agreement was concluded between the AESD and the Engineering Employers' Federation in 1924. This spelt out that the only people who would be recognised for negotiating purposes were draughtsmen, calculators, estimators and tracers. Chief Draughtsmen and Assistant Chiefs were excluded. In 1935 the Agreement included apprentices. Planning Engineers (properly qualified ie. ex-draughtsmen) were included in 1944. When an agreement on minimum rates was reached only those categories listed benefited. It was obvious that draughtsmen would have a vested interested in maintaining a minimum rates agreement. The "technicians whose function was related to design" would either have to take very vigorous action for recognition or be satisfied with what they could get from consequential adjustments following on a settlement of a drawing office review. In many cases these consequentially were marginal or non-existent.

SIDE BY CLYDE... Scottish workers at Singer's, take their strike onto the streets of Glasgow.

A report by the Executive Committee to the 1962 Conference indicated the steps which were being taken to deal with this problem. Several meetings had taken place between representatives of the Association and the Engineering Employers' Federation to consider alterations in the Procedure Agreement arising from the change of title and rules. The Federation was having none of it. Recognising DATA for staff other than draughtsmen would, in the opinion of the employers, be counter productive.

Faced with what it saw as downright recalcitrance the Executive Committee came back to the 1963 Conference with a declaration of guerilla war. It said "The Executive Committee undertakes to give what support is necessary, including permission for strike action and financial support if need be, to members who are eligible under Rules but who are denied the right to collective bargaining by their employers or by employers' organisations".

DATA had already demonstrated that it was not given to making idle threats. At the Blackburn Aircraft Co of Brough, it had supported nearly 400 members in a six-week strike which resulted in substantial increases for draughtsmen, estimators, planning engineers and tracers and improvements for apprentices. The company further agreed to set up new salary scales for "other technicians".

1964 saw no change in the employers' position nationally. There was in that year another breakthrough at Bristol Siddley Engines where a large number of members, not covered by the National Procedure, achieved similar increases to those conceded to the normally recognised groups. Once again the Executive Committee made it clear it would back any technician members who were prepared to go on strike for recognition.

To say "this one will run" would be an understatement when it came to the Association's claim that the national negotiating procedure agreement should be extended to include "Allied Technicans". Right through the sixties and into the seventies, when the union had once again changed its name and become a section of the Amalgamated Union of Engineering Workers, it was still a bone of contention.

Some advance was recorded in 1969 when, as the report said "after lengthy discussions, it was finally agreed the Weights Engineers, Standards and Spares Engineers, Technical Authors and Technical Illustrators would be covered." The Report went on "and since their technical competency is equivalent to that of other classes covered the same minimum salaries would apply." The question being begged was, who decided the level of technical competency to which nationally agreed minimum rates should apply? Then just to add another ingredient to the conjecture over recognition was the considerable presence of other white collar unions and the white collar sections of manual unions who were also laying claim to represent technicians whether "allied" or not. A case in point was the serious dispute at C A Parsons Ltd of Newcastle- Upon-Tyne. Here was a company where increases in pay achieved by DATA, sometimes through taking industrial action, were applied to all other technical staff whether they were members or not. In 1969 the DATA representatives considered it would be sensible to approach the management for a formal agreement through which the Association could represent all technical staff. Faced with the reality of the situation the management concurred. Then some technical staff members, who had always benefited from DATA settlements but who stayed out of the union, decided that being represented by mere draughtsmen was infra dig. Using a procedure which had been granted to the Association of Scientific Workers which amalgamated with the Association of Supervisory Staffs Executive and Technicians to become the Association of Scientific, Technical and Managerial Staff, they persuaded the company to concede recognition to ASTMS.

As would be expected DATA's protests at a flagrant breach of a signed agreement were vigorous. In the end nearly 200 members were locked out. This was a nasty one not only because it involved another TUC union but because of the implications it would have on other engineering companies. A dispute over the same kind of issues was taking place at the Birmingham based Pressed Steel Fisher Co Ltd.

Over a period of months with C A Parson's members still out on the street, DATA took part in a complicated series of negotiations which involved the Engineers Employers' Federation, the TUC and the Department of Employment. What came out at the end was an agreement which gave DATA exclusive negotiating rights for the whole of the technical staff and established a closed shop to commence twelve months after the agreement was signed.

This was one of the most significant breakthroughs on the question of extending recognition beyond the drawing office in a very important company. The terms of settlement were observed throughout the Parsons Reyrolle Peebles Group. The aftermath did, however, contain the seeds of some future contentious matters which DATA would have to live with.

No employers' organisation was more resolute in its refusal to give DATA credibility anywhere other than in the drawing office than the Shipbuilding Employers' Federation. When the AESD tried to get formal recognition in 1940 it met with a blank refusal. The then General Secretary, James Young, was able to enlist the help of Ernest Bevin, the Minister of Labour, who managed to persuade the employers to think again. In 1941 a National Agreement giving the Association the right to negotiate on behalf of draughtsmen was signed. And as far as these employers were concerned that meant draughtsmen and nobody else.

Twenty-five years later the Shipbuilding Employers were moved to consider including planning engineers in the Agreement, something the Engineering Employers had conceded in 1944. Then in 1967 came the shipbuilding lockout and the Agreement remained in its 1941 form for another two years. By this time the Engineering Employers had revised their National Agreement to include five further categories - weights engineers, spares engineers, technical authors, technical illustrators and standards engineers. True to form the shipbuilding employers waited until 1971 before coming in line.

As far as the Association was concerned things were better ordered in individual yards. At the Fairfield Yard in Glasgow DATA had been granted sole negotiating rights for virtually all technical staff. It was significant that Fairfields was not a member of the Employers' Federation. It became part of the Upper Clyde Consortium in 1968 and then under British Shipbuilders it was renamed Govan Shipbuilders. It was also significant that many of the most active members at local, regional and national level were employed in this yard.

Similar sole negotiating rights Agreements were in operation at the Swan Hunter North East coast yards, at Brooke Marine in Lowestoft, on the south coast at Vosper-Thornycroft and at Vickers and Cammel Lairds on the Mersey.

In order to recruit and retain suitably qualified technical staff those companies which were not members of the Engineering Employers' Federation were willing to apply at least the DATA/EEF agreed improvements in pay and conditions. In many of these firms DATA had negotiated better and more accommodating agreements than that with the EEF.

The left wing activists who had persuaded the policy making conference and the EC back in the mid-forties to go for a National Minimum Rate Agreement were now thinking of ways to get out of it. To those technicians who were not covered by the procedure agreement, minimum rates, no matter how good, were irrelevant. Yet these were the categories that DATA wanted to recruit. But there was no way the draughtsmen, still the largest and most influential group, would be prepared to give up what they saw was the main reason for being a union at all. And just to make matters more complicated for the left there was the political levy that justified the battles for higher rates of pay - a frontal attack on the capitalist system and a practical lesson to those involved in the irreconcilable clash of interests between employees and employers. To some traditionally-minded members it seemed like the Association was being asked to throw away a winning hand and still scoop the pool.

In 1971, ten years after it had been decided that the union should venture outside the drawing office, a motion was passed at the Annual Conference saying that now that it had amalgamated with the AEF it ought to be giving guidance on wages and conditions to staff whose jobs were not related to design. On behalf of the EC, Ken Gill the then Editor, supported the proposal. He said that up until now caution had been necessary because of lack of practical experience in negotiating for these new areas of membership but that now there was sufficient record and experiences to give real guidance. Through its system of collecting statistics on pay and conditions direct from the members the union did have an impressive accumulation of useful information. The Engineering Employers had in the meantime rejected the union's claim for improvements in the minimum rates. So with no National Agreement the battle would have to take place at the plants. Showing some concern over what this might cost in strike pay the EC indicated it would be more inclined to support those who were in the lower pay ranges...which it did.

The debate at Conference in 1972 was on a traditional motion asking the EC to publish and pursue the implementation of a new minimum wage for age scale. There were eleven amendments to be gone through before the final figures were agreed. These were £33 per week at the age of 20 to £40.50 per week at 30 for the procedurally recognised categories. No one mentioned "the not related to design". A chink in enlightenment showed in 1973 when it was agreed that the union should continue to publish minimum rates but that these ought to reflect the broad base of the membership. Another motion saying that too much attention was attached to minimum rates and they they should be played down failed to get carried. A year later the EC decided to amend a proposal that called for the future minimum rates scales not to go beyond the age of 25. The EC amendment was for the continuance of the scale up to the age of 30. Jack Carr, who was moving the amendment on behalf of the EC, informed the delegates that if this amendment was defeated then the EC would support a new scale stopping at 25. Apparently he was testing the water. The amendment was defeated. New rates were declared up to the age of 25. The delegates also agreed with the sentiments in a motion that said in a good many words that scales on pay should be determined for all categories of members as a matter of urgency.

In the middle of 1976 TASS News published target salaries in which the rates of the traditional members were taken as benchmarks around which other job titles were slotted in. For the first time there was no debate on minimum rates at the Annual Conference, instead a reaffirmation of the intention to develop the flexibility that would allow the needs of all members to be taken into consideration. After over 30 years of extremely active life the minimum wage campaign was buried.

As a result of discussions with the Engineering Employers' Federation a formula was found to resolve the question of recognising TASS outside its traditional areas. It was carefully worded and universal in application. It said "where a union not entitled to recognition under a National Procedure Agreement for a grade of staff which is agreed to be an appropriate level of staff for collective recognition has a significant presence and is a major influence in the grade, the Federation will generally advise that recognition shall not be withheld".

The words epitomised the cautious way in which the Federation approached an accommodation when it had to.

the shipbuilders' lockout

Whether it was because draughtsmen employed by a shipbuilder started the union in the first place or whether it was because some of the most articulate, politically motivated activists worked in the industry, the relationship between DATA and the Shipbuilding Employers Federation (SEF) was, to say the least, fragile.

The SEF consistently refused to have any truck with the Draughtsmen's Association about a wage-for-age scale of minimum rates. The consequence of this situation was the increased demand by the draughtsmen for the Association to do something about it. They complained that they were getting a raw deal, that their living standards were falling and they knew the industry was having difficulty in recruiting experienced draughtsmen. Allowing for wage claim rhetoric, there was evidence that what they were saying had more than a grain of truth.

Following on a resolution passed at the 1964 Annual Conference of the Representative Council, the Executive Committee went to the employers with its usual well researched and documented claim. The view it put forward was that it would be in the best interests of shipbuilding if a scale of minimum rates was agreed. Barely pausing to glance at the Association's arithmetic the SEF placed their own version of a wage scale on the table. It was much lower than the Association's and it had strings - rises only for those below what they were offering and no more claims at any individual yard. It was a reply guaranteed to lead to an industrial stand-off.

For starters, the draughtsmen tried an overtime ban and a few token stoppages. The employers were unimpressed. Then at five selected yards the DATA membership came out on strike. This time the employers did respond. They said if the strikers did not return to work forthwith they would suspend every DATA member in the industry - a lockout in other words. It was quite obvious that tempers were rising on both sides and a damaging confrontation was on the way. Mr G Brown, the newly appointed Minister decided to intervene. He invited representatives from both sides to meet officials of his Department to see if there was any chance of a compromise settlement. The employers still insisted they would not go beyond what they had offered. That, replied the union representatives, was not acceptable. Nor was the suggestion that the issue should be referred to the newly formed "Prices and Incomes Review Board". And in line with its stated policy that disputes of this nature were best settled by negotiation between the parties concerned DATA rejected the idea of arbitration.

Seeing that he was getting nowhere as a conciliator the Minister indicated that a Court of Inquiry could be set up to examine the case and make recommendations. A precondition for such a hearing would be that both sides would call off their action. The DATA Executive Committee held one of its soul-searching meetings and after hours of agonising decided to ballot the shipyard membership with a recommendation that they should go ahead and submit evidence to the Court of Inquiry. After all, they claimed they had a good case so there was nothing to lose by stating it in public. At a few shipyards the more militant members argued hotly that the union should have nothing to do with these legal shenanigans, at the others the majority view was that they should submit their case.

To the surprise of the cynics the report from the Court of Inquiry upheld many of the points from the DATA submission. Wages, it agreed, were low in comparison to those in the broader engineering industry. Low pay was a factor which inhibited recruitment from the shopfloor where an apprentice would be better off remaining on the tools rather than studying for a job in the drawing office. The Court saw no objection to the introduction of a wage-for-age pay scale that established minimum rates up to the age of 30. Nor did it see anything wrong with individual groups of members making a case for rates which were above such a scale. The Court could not accept that everybody should be tied to the minimum standard.

The two sides were advised to return to the negotiating table and see if they could reach agreement taking account of the Court's recommendations. After the predictable "lengthy meetings" DATA and the SEF reached an agreement for a scale of minimum rates. The agreement gave a 21 year old £15 per week and rose to £22.50 for those aged 30 and over. For tracers the 16 year old got £6 per week rising to £12.75 at the age of 25. An additional £1 per week was given to everyone working within a 25-mile radius of Charing Cross, London. It took a little longer to settle the rates for apprentices and junior tracers. Negotiations were going on with the Engineering Employers at the same time to try and get the apprentice rate related to that of the time-served draughtsmen. In the end all parties agreed to allow the matter to go to Arbitration. The arbitration award was that apprentice rates should be related in percentage terms to those of a 21 year old draughtsman on minimum rates. The junior tracers got increases in proportion to the main settlements but the employers would not accept that there was any need for a national agreement on rates for trainee tracers.

Thus the unpleasantness ended, or did it? For a while there was a period which could be described as a "cold truce". It lasted until 27 February 1967. On that date 168 DATA members at Swan Hunter and Wigham Richardson Ltd, having failed to get a satisfactory response to a claim for improved rates through the negotiating procedure, withdrew their labour. They were backed by the Executive Committee.

Perhaps it was because Mr N Sloan QC, Director of the Shipbuilding Employers' Federation was a Scot and felt doubly disaffected with the Draughtsmen's Union or, perhaps, it was because the employers had an unused lockout notice left over from the last time, they promptly notified George Doughty that if the draughtsmen at Swan Hunter did not return to work by 8 March they would suspend every DATA member in the industry.

Normally, employers can do without a strike. When one happens, just like trade unions, those in the industry affected will close ranks to the extent that they will assert support for the one in trouble. Again, like unions, they will be careful not to be so committed that they might bring economic hardship on themselves. Yet, here were the shipbuilding

LOUDER THAN WORDS... 1965 shipyard lockouts on Clydeside, top, **and Tyneside,** above, **provoke swift action.**

employers who in day-to-day business were in competition with each other being willing to provoke disputes in their individual firms because one of their number had a problem. As Arthur Scott, a leading activist at Swan Hunter and later the President of the Union said at the time of the 1965 lockout threat "We give the SEF a bit of a toothache and to cure it they have decided to cut off their own head".

Decapitation or not the SEF was obviously spoiling for a fight. It must have considered that the Association would not be able to support so many members on strike pay for too long, that it would be bled of funds. As it happened they guessed wrong.

At a meeting on 1 March the DATA EC seething with indignation claimed that not only was this a breach of the procedure agreement but also a breach of the contract of employment of those who were carrying out normal duties. In an angry statement the Executive Committee made it clear that "it was not prepared to capitulate to such bullying attacks and it would not be in order for members at Swan Hunter to return to work until a satisfactory offer was made". It further issued an instruction to the members in the other shipyards to report for work as usual on 8 March. If the employer refused them admission the EC would support them at 80 per cent of their normal take home pay.

To show that it was going to put its money where its mouth was the Association indicated it would use all its liquid assets if that were necessary. It would enter into loans/mortgages to obtain extra finances. A levy which doubled the members' normal subscriptions rate would be introduced and appeals for donations would be circulated throughout the labour and trade union movement. The response to all these appeals was very encouraging. Resolutions of support poured in from branches all over the country. The trade unions in the shipbuilding and engineering industries were generous in their contributions to the DATA fighting fund. District Committees all over the country and trades councils pitched in with financial help and messages of support. Many groups of DATA members organised special collections and reports were coming in of members voluntarily increasing their subscriptions over and above the official levy.

An unlooked for consequence of this dispute, as far as the employers were concerned, was the growing rapport between DATA activists and the manual workers' shop stewards. This was something which was going to influence the outcome of the exploratory discussions taking place with the main engineering union, the AEF, on a possible amalgamation.

The employers calling on their historical experience announced that any DATA members who wished to be put back on the payroll would have to sign a document disassociating themselves from the union. As far as was known, two did. Then Mr N Sloan QC, with breathtaking gall suggested that if the Swan Hunter people returned to work the other shipbuilding employers would reciprocate by allowing their staff to come back as well. The strike solidified.

With both sides under a lot of pressure from the Minister of Labour and officials of the TUC, DATA insisted there could be no talks with Swan Hunter until the lockout was called off. The employers caved in and on 15 May all the shipbuilding DATA members returned to their jobs. Within hours of the starting time on the same day, negotiations began at Wallsend with the DATA representatives and the Swan Hunter management. The terms which were initially put on the table to get a return to work applied to draughtsmen only. By the time the negotiations were completed and agreement reached, senior draughtsmen, section leaders, planning engineers and tracers all gained substantial increases. Into the bargain Swan Hunter conceded for the first time a wage-for-age scale of minimum rates up to the age of 30.

On 16 May, thirteen weeks after the start of the strike, the Swan Hunter members lined up in the morning before starting time and with banner flying marched in procession through the shipyard gates. They had all come out together and that was the way they went back.

In the tidying-up process DATA tried to get the employers to pay up the back contributions to the company pension scheme and the outstanding social security contributions. This the employers refused to do. They were, however, persuaded to restore two public holidays which were lost during the strike. There was a decision by a Local Appeals Tribunal on the north east coast not to allow unemployment benefit to two named test cases. DATA engaged a Counsel to represent the members at a further appeal to the National Commissioner. This lawyer advised the Association not to bother making a case as the hearing would be merely concerned with points of law. He was wrong. The Commissioner rejected the appeal on the grounds that having only heard the argument made by the employers he had to assume it was true.

Another two test cases were brought before the Commissioner at Belfast. This time the Association provided evidence and was successful.

As soon as the increases achieved at Swan Hunter became known throughout the rest of the shipbuilding membership claims were made domestically for similar treatment. Knowing the mood of the members as a result of their lockout experience the employers were obliged to concede. Although the Association had never intended the Swan Hunter issue to be the forerunner of a national wage claim that is the way it turned out in the end.

DATA's status in the trade union movement was enhanced by its ability to hold out against a powerful employers' organisation. In financial terms the union spent £250,000 on the dispute but it received a remarkable £110,000 in levies and donations which showed how well the membership had been mobilised in support of the action. Then there were the very useful and positive relationships which so many groups established with the shopfloor unions.

But success often inflates expectations. Those who imagined DATA was an instrument of political, economic and social reform took from the lockout a confirmation of their theory that capitalism could be brought down through militant activity at the workplace. The political factions within DATA were now tripartite, the right, the left and the ultra left. Connoisseurs were intrigued by the areas of overlap.

Rookes v Barnard

It was a primary aim of DATA to secure 100 per cent membership agreements. This would mean that although non-members could be offered jobs in firms or in departments of firms where DATA was recognised as the negotiating body for the employees concerned, it was a condition of employment that they would join the union. This was a less severe arrangement than the manual union pre-entry closed shop. In the companies with a high density of DATA members there was rarely any difficulty in obtaining such an agreement. The convenience of procuring agreements on pay and conditions for all staff employees was acknowledged by both sides. It seemed fair and logical that applicants who were willing to accept a job for which pay and conditions were negotiated by the Association should be part of that collective. DATA members in general had little time for the free riders, those who were glad to accept the terms which others had struggled to obtain but who felt no obligation to contribute to those efforts. The opposers of 100 per cent membership agreements redefined democracy, as the right of the individual to reject the view of the majority.

In 1955 the AESD had a registered 100 per cent membership agreement at the design office of British Overseas Airways Corporation, which was located at London Airport. "Registered" in the BOAC context meant that the management acknowledged the fact that there was 100 per cent trade union membership in the office and that it would do nothing to interfere with that arrangement. One of the AESD committee members who had secured the arrangement was a Mr Rookes. As occasionally happens in even the best intentioned firms an issue arose over which the Association and the management were at odds. Mr Rookes was all for taking "direct action" to deal with the matter. The full-time official of the AESD, Mr R Silverthorne, advised against this and urged the proper way to handle the grievance was through the BOAC negotiating procedure. Mr Rookes would have none of it. A meeting of the members was held and by a substantial majority they accepted the advise of Mr Silverthorne. "Because" as the Chairman of BOAC, Sir Miles Thomas put it, "he was unable to persuade it to dance to his tune," Mr Rookes resigned from the Association. No amount of discussion could make him change his mind. The registered agreement was no longer 100 per cent.

Having failed to get Mr Rookes to reconsider his action the members decided to apply some pressure on the management. They delivered an ultimatum saying that if Mr Rookes was not removed from the office before a certain date the rest of them would withdraw their labour. The management, clearly upset at the way things were heading, asked the members to retract the strike threat and allow further talks to take place. This was agreed but, unfortunately, the situation remained unaltered, nobody was prepared to make any concessions. Finally, in a bid for some sort of peace the management firstly suspended Mr Rookes and then in March 1956 gave him the appropriate notice of dismissal.

Mr Rookes was far from finished. He took legal advice and in 1957 sued three of the Association's representatives for damages on the grounds that they had wrongfully induced BOAC to sack him from his job. The three people named were the Divisional Organiser Mr R Silverthorne, the Branch Chairman Mr A Barnard and the Corresponding Member Mr T J Fistal. The Executive Committee, having consulted its own legal advisors, was able to provide legal assistance to the three defendants because the affair arose during a trade dispute and, therefore, their action would not be illegal under the 1906 Trades Dispute Act. As written, the Act seemed to say that if anyone is induced to break a contract of employment or if trade or business suffers because of an industrial dispute there is no redress for damages in law. The Association was to learn that the Act said what certain judges said it said.

Mr Rookes argued that the threat of strike action issued by the AESD representatives was a breach of the "no-strike" clause of the BOAC procedure agreement and that, therefore, they had acted illegally. The case reached the High Court in 1961. The hearing lasted two weeks. The judge, Mr Justice Sachs, spent the whole day summing up and the jury found for the plaintiff. Damages totalling £7,500 were awarded against the defendents. The manner in which this judge had interpreted the 1906 Act caused concern not only for the Association but also for the whole trade union movement. Notice of Appeal was submitted. Mr Justice Sachs ordered that £2,500 be deposited in the court pending the appeal.

The rules of the union at the time would not allow legal damages to be paid from its funds. It could, however, pay the costs. To assist the defendants each was given a benevolent grant of £500 and an appeal was launched for voluntary donations. It brought in, mostly from other trade union members and Labour Party constituencies, another £5,000. A loan from the Association's funds of £1,000 was advanced by the Executive Committee and later refunded from the proceeds of a collection which the EC had organised.

Gerald Gardiner QC, was retained to represent the three members at the hearing of the appeal on 9 February 1962. This time the Court of Appeal reversed the findings of the High Court and the Association and the defendants thought they were in the clear. Mr Rookes had demonstrated he was not one to be put off just because people took decisions against him. The House of Lords was available and so that was where he took his case.

The Lords deliberated during November and December 1963. To the absolute horror of the Association they upheld Mr Rookes' appeal and found Messrs Barnard, Silverthorne and Fistal guilty as in the High Court. They also ordered a new trial to be held on the question of the amount of compensation. What followed was a series of legal exchanges like chess players quickly clearing the board to get to the end game. The new trial was set to be heard by a jury in February 1965. The Association's lawyers asked for a trial by a judge. The Master of the Rolls agreed. Mr Rookes' solicitors successfully appealed against this. The Association was then advised by Counsel to pay £4,000 into the Court. Once again Mr Rooks' solicitors challenged and tried to get an increase on this figure. Then, just before the new trial was due to take place, Mr Rookes agreed to accept the money, in full settle-

J E Mortimer, tireless campaigner whose efforts bore fruit in the shape of the 1965 Trade Disputes Bill.

ment of his claim. The eight years of litigation had come to an end. The Association had to pay the costs.

Through the generosity of the British labour movement the collection organised by the Executive Committee raised £16,000. DATA acknowledged the help which came from among many others, prominent unions such as the Iron and Steel Trades Confederation, The National Union of General and Municipal Workers, The National Union of Sheet Metal Workers and Coppersmiths, The National Union of Journalists, The National Union of Public Employees, The Merchant Navy and Airline Officers Associations. There were contributions from the agricultural workers, the print workers, the firemen and from virtually every organisation in the Confederation of Shipbuilding and Engineering Unions. The complete list was an impressive indication of the concern being felt over their Lordships' interpretation of the 1906 Act.

The DATA Executive Committee saw the flimsiness of the trades unions' reliance on immunity under the law for actions taken in order to concentrate the minds of employers on the claims and grievances of their members. It had never occurred to even the most experienced lawyers that the Law Lords could dig up what one Appeal Judge called "this obscure, unfamilar and peculiar wrong". The decision from the House of Lords at the Rookes v Barnard Appeal was that the threat to break a "no-strike" clause in the agreement between the employers and employees was a civil wrong or "intimidation". This ruling meant that any union threatening to take industrial action which would break the members' contract of employment would be guilty of "intimidation" and, therefore, they could be sued for damages.

Indeed, they could even be sued by a third party who might claim they suffered injury due to the industrial action. In strict legal terms unions were free to organise and to pursue issues on behalf of their members but if it became necessary to take strike action and the members contract of employment was broken (as it always would be in any kind of industrial action) then they would be actionable by law.

As far as trade unions were concerned Rookes v Barnard had sown a real legal minefield. It took time, but through tireless campaigning, especially by George Doughty and J E Mortimer in the TUC, the CSEU and the Labour Party, joint union lobbies of sponsored MPs resulted in the 1965 Trade Disputes Bill. This Bill intended to restore the traditional immunities against legal action which unions thought they had.

It far from satisfied the DATA EC who were campaigning for positive legal rights rather than the negative right not to be sued in court for doing what they always did when negotiations with an employer broke down.

Significantly, when the Bill was going through the House of Commons, 120 Conservative MPs signed a motion to change the law in such a way that the Law Lords ruling would be a permanent fixture in future trade union legislation. What could be described as Tory prescience.

scientific workers and civil servants

J E Mortimer, in the concluding chapter of the History of the AESD, referred to the desirability of the members of the Draughtsmen's Association and those of the Association of Scientific Workers (ASCW) co-operating with each other in certain firms where both organisations had a presence.

Talks about talks on a possible merger between the two Associations began taking place during 1959/60. What was designated as a pilot scheme to encourage a closer working relationship was tried out in Sheffield and the West Riding areas of Yorkshire. The idea was that they would make joint representations to their employers with the lead being taken by the larger group.

In 1963 the ASCW claimed that there was a certain amount of hostility among its rank and file to the idea of amalgamation with anyone. They proposed instead a federation of themselves with DATA and ASSET. This proposal did not get off the ground simply because there already was a white collar union Joint Council of Staff Unions which allowed these bodies to liaise as much as they liked. Nevertheless, the Associations kept in touch and maintained fraternal contact.

1966 saw a big effort to resolve the merger question once and for all. The ASCW now had on its table resolutions concerning possible amalgamations. Two of these called for joining the DATA, two wanted talks with DATA and ASSET and one wanted talks with ASSET alone. Mr J Dutton, General Secretary, and Dr W A Wooster, the incoming President attended the DATA Annual Conference. Both George Doughty and Dr Wooster took the opportunity to make statements which conveyed their profoundest hopes that the two associations would find a formula which would allow them to come together in one fold. Both speakers were heartily applauded by the Conference delegates. Arrangements were made for the two Executive Committees to get together and find that accommodation.

The answer to those aspirations came in the last week of April 1967 at the Annual Conference of the DATA Representative Council. A report of the outcome of the negotiations between the ECs of the two Associations was presented to the delegates by the Vice President, A McTurk. He assured the Conference that the EC had gone into the talks with enthusiasm and high hopes of fruitful and purposeful negotiations. It commenced a close examination of the small print and found there were details of structure and attitude which would be very difficult to resolve. DATA was a union with a militant policy and was always willing to take employers on if they failed to negotiate an acceptable agreement. The DATA rate of subscriptions for membership were set at a level to allow that policy to be continued. There were sections of the ASCW where the likelihood of strike action was, to say the least, remote, the medical technicans, for example. ASCW representatives thought those members should have a lower subscription rate. DATA representatives thought it might be possible to accommodate them on this issue, if it were only the medical technicans involved. But the ASCW had members in the education services for whom strike action would be equally improbable. What about the lower subscription for these? DATA's reply was that this group was so badly paid that strike action would be the only effective way of dealing with that situation, therefore they should pay the full subscription!

The next problem was the number of ASCW officials added to the number of DATA officials. The would be, in DATA's opinion, excessive for the needs of the amalgamated union and into the bargain there was no way DATA would wear the ASCW proposal of a Joint General Secretaryship.

In terms of the proposed structure of the amalgamated union DATA made it clear it was talking about an engineering industry union with a service industry section. That would mean a proportionally smaller number of ASCW representatives on the Joint Executive Committee. This did not please the ASCW either. When the idea of an alternating president for the amalgamated union was floated the DATA negotiators sank it with emphasis on the weight of responsibilities the president would have to carry, meaning the job was, in practice, full time. The difficulty the two sides found in arranging meetings was due to the ASCW representatives not being able to get time off from work. The alternating presidency looked like a non-starter too.

There was nothing obscure about the message Mr McTurk was putting across. He concluded his report by referring to an emergency motion from the EC. The reason for this procedure was that the ASCW had just completed its own annual conference and had resolved, in view of the problems arising in the talks with DATA, they saw no point in pursuing the issue any further. It was up to DATA to make its reply. The emergency motion did this. What it said in essence was that because of the dissimilarities between the two unions any further concession by DATA would damage the interests of its membership. Continuing the discussions would be, in the opinion of the EC, fruitless. There were no hard feelings. In those firms where they both had members co-operation would continue.

At this point J E Mortimer, who was at the time Editor of DATA Journal, intervened to explain why he did not go along with his colleagues with regard to reducing subscriptions for the medical technicans in ASCW. He thought this was too much of a concession. He agreed with the conclusion reached in the report that the question of further discussion was no longer worth pursuing but he felt it should be put on record that as far as he was concerned the idea of DATA having a "no-strike" section was "unacceptable." "It is bad trade unionism" he said. At the back of his mind Jim Mortimer also feared that bringing the ASCW into DATA would put paid to any further talks on what he believed was the more logical amalgamation with the AEU.

As it happened not everybody was convinced by the tone of this motion. An amendment appeared in the names of Harlow and Whetstone branches. Their complaint was that both sides were being far too rigid and that it should be possible to make further modifications to the DATA position without jeopardising the interests of the members. The amendment went on to suggest that the negotiations should be reopened.

The proposer and seconder of the amendment

put their case on the basis of technological developments in industry with particular emphasis on what was happening in the field of electronics. They argued that the future designers were as likely to be in the laboratory as the drawing office. A broad-based technical union was essential to meet the needs of a growing industrial workforce. The recruitment potential in the technician categories was, in their opinion, enormous. Nobody was denying that parts of the ASCW were backward but joining with DATA would help to bring them along. As the seconder from Whetstone put it, "trade unionism is like swimming - if you do not participate regularly, when you do try you find yourself all sore and stiff afterwards and less inclined to try."

By coincidence the two speakers who supported the amendment were both called Harry Smith. One, a Yorkshireman and at the time a Divisional Organiser, was a member of the Communist Party. He had a further distinction in that in 1960/61 he was the last President of the AESD and the first President of DATA. The other who died in 1986, was the EC member for South East London, a Labour Councillor but said by many to hold very right wing views. Harry Smith, the Divisional Organiser; a man with powerful oratorical gifts, laid into Jim Mortimer's statement about a no-strike policy being bad trade unionism. "Militant trade unionism" he told the delegates "varies in content and is related to particular circumstances." Having drawn a dramatic picture of a child dying in hospital because the medical technicians were on strike he turned to Jim Mortimer and declaimed "bring some humanity and sensitivity to the points you are holding as slogans for the movement."

London's Harry Smith, on the other hand, was far less altruistic. "Bend over backwards to come to some arrangement but after you have got them then convince them that our way of approach is the correct one."

Neither of the Smiths got any support and George Doughty chided the full-time official for doubting the tolerance and humanity of the DATA negotiators. He reminded Conference of the brave concessions they had made: accepting the principle of graded subscriptions "with great trepidation at what this Conference might say."

The amendment, needless to say, was soundly defeated and the EC's emergency motion carried. Two weeks later the ASCW announced it had amalgamated with ASSET and together they formed ASTMS. Clive Jenkins, the General Secretary of ASSET, became the leader of ASTMS. Clearly, ASSET had taken heed of Harry Smith's course of action and convinced ASCW that its way was better.

DATA's chances of doing a deal with the Society of Technical Civil Servants (STCS) looked better. This body had, like the ASCW, a friendly relationship with the AESD since its foundation in 1946. In 1957 it agreed to an arrangement for sharing services with DATA. There were exchanges of publications, joint delegations and representatives of each organisation attending the other's formal meetings.

In 1965 they were really getting down to it. Proposals in regard to the integration of subscriptions, membership records and benefits were well advanced. Everything looked set for a successful merger. 1966 and the talk was about the setting up of a public services section of DATA with a public services committee which would have a great deal of autonomy and would report to the DATA Executive Committee. It was all over bar the signing. Some tying of loose ends took place in 1967, the arrangements for the Technical Civil Servants in relation to collective bargaining and the procedures which would allow for their sectional identity within the merged organisation. An eight-man delegation of the STCS at the DATA 1967 Annual Conference heard A McTurk welcoming them to the Conference and inviting them to participate in the debates (without a vote, of course) and also reminding the Conference of their long and fruitful association with each other. He did mention that a committee, under the chairmanship of one Sir John Scott Fulton (later Baron Fulton) was looking into the structure of the whole Civil Service and that it would be wise to await its report before finalising the amalgamation agreement.

The years rolled on and at the 1969 DATA Conference a ten-man delegation from the STCS took their now accustomed place as honourary (non-voting) delegates, patiently waiting for the Fulton Report before they consummated their merger with the main body.

At last the Fulton Committee deliberations were made known to those long- suffering interested parties. In short, it said public servants should be in a Public Servants' Union. This time the 1969 DATA Conference had a nine-man and one-women delegation. Now the issue of amalgamation was suspended while the implications of Fulton were examined. Both the Society and the Association continued to reassure each other that they were still good friends.

The conclusions of Fulton were not good. A single delegate from the Society at the 1970 Conference heard the EC report that as a result of the civil service re-organisation proposals the STCS members had voted for a merger into the Institute of Professional Civil Servants and in three years' time it would cease to exist. In view of this the DATA EC was of the opinion that there was no reason for not having a friendly relationship with the IPCS but that the special arrangements which had existed in the past with the STCS should now be terminated.

What would have happened had DATA and the STCS taken the opportunity of amalgamation before Fulton remains an intriguing speculation.

the 1970 Rolls-Royce dispute

The leadership of DATA concluded that the days when it could support long drawn out strikes were coming to an end. Even with the strike benefit reduced to 60 per cent of take home pay the financial strain was a cause of concern. The message to the membership was, continue pressing the claims but try to contrive more economic methods of doing so.

Draughtsmen were never short of imagination. They soon began to devise novel methods for concentrating the minds of the management on their problems. The idea was to resolve deadlock situations by taking industrial action involving a minimum cost to the union while at the same time posing a threat to the continuity of production. For example, in firms with a large membership a small number from a vital production area would withdraw their labour and be supported by a voluntary levy from those who remained at work.

Overtime bans and the refusal to handle work done by outside contractors were considered to be very mundane tactics by some of the more inventive groups. For these, pressurising the management called for more sophisticated stratagems. "Working without enthusiasm" became a by-word in the well organised firms where the negotiating committees were meeting resistance in carrying out the behests of the membership.

The simpler forms of unenthusiastic working included refusing to answer internal telephone calls, sending memos with queries through the company mailing system to people who worked only a few feet away, redrawing plans completely instead of using an eraser to make a small alteration. When negotiations seemed to be getting nowhere "spontaneous" token stoppages would take place. Members would, with military precision, leave their workplaces, don their outdoor clothes and march away from the premises. Sometimes they would march back inside an hour, sometimes they would not return until the following morning. Those who had a flair for the more dramatic demonstrations would arrange "think-ins". Every single members would come in to work, sit at the drawing board and stare into space. When managers eventually noticed that no work was being done and began to kick up a row they would be told that draughtsmen were paid to draw and to think - "today they were thinking." It was claimed that in a large drawing office in the North of England a queue formed the length of the office when everybody decided to go to the loo at the same time. It was alleged that at one company a chief draughtsman stormed out of his office when he noticed every single member was at his drawing board, head down, working busily. "You're working to rule" he shouted, "I know you are". Normal working as far as he was concerned meant some people at their appropriate place, some others away

AIRING GRIEVANCES... Mike Cooley, third from right, **and Grenvile Clay,** second from right, **with Rolls-Royce workers lobby the TUC with the support of Heathrow Airport workers in 1967.**

from their boards having a chat and the odd one or two slipping out for a smoke.

Personnel Managers deplored these actions, they were irritating and in their eyes childish. Nevertheless, they were a means of showing serious dissatisfaction and an indication that the issue in contention had the backing of the full membership. The ultimate aim was to get the matter dealt with without an all- out strike.

The Engineering Employers' Federation was naturally concerned over what some commentators were calling "DATA's guerilla tactics". It dawned on them that the Achilles heel of this tough union may be its financial resources. The Federation's policy would be to support a company that could tolerate a strike or a lockout for long enough to put the union under unacceptable financial stress.

In 1969 a bitter dispute lasting the best part of three months had taken place at the Rolls-Royce plant in Hillington near Glasgow. These very militant and well-organised DATA members squeezed out a £3 per week across the board increase. The knock-on forced the Employers' Federation to conclude a National Minimum Rate Agreement at a much higher level than it wanted. This denouement rankled the Rolls-Royce management and the Federation.

When the local agreement between DATA and Rolls-Royce, Coventry came to an end in July 1970 the stage was set for the battle to be renewed. This time the management at Coventry made up its mind not to suffer a repeat of the Hillington performance. The Engineering Employers' Federation was determined to give the company all the help it could.

There were 970 DATA members employed at the Coventry plant. On their behalf the office committee submitted a claim for a substantial increase. The management response was a take-it-or-leave-it offer of 7 per cent with strings attached. The strings included changes in work practice that had never been discussed before.

The offer was rejected and the management was told to try again. This resulted in the offer being confirmed with the conditions unchanged and a statement that the same offer would be made to every group of members throughout the Rolls-Royce organisation. The Coventry members applied an overtime ban and withdrew 24 specialists from a key department.

A number of angry meetings took place at which the company side threatened to lock out the whole membership if it persisted in refusing its offer. Which is exactly what happened and DATA found itself supporting nearly 1,000 members on 60 per cent of normal take home pay. The EC called on the total membership to pay a levy of up to 25p per week.

After about eight weeks the company took the unusual step of invoking the National Procedure Agreement. This allowed them to arrange a Conference at which they, along with the representatives of the Engineering Employers' Federation, could talk to the national officials of the union.

Every group of DATA members within the Rolls-Royce combine was included in the procedure. In the end a formal failure to agree was registered with respect to each group except Derby. With nothing fresh to put on the table this peculiar exercise must have been intended to give the Federation representatives a whiff of the firing line.

After a series of abortive informal meetings the Rolls-Royce management decided to up the ante. An ultimatum was issued stating that unless the DATA members at every plant accepted the 7 per cent and undertook to do the work not being done due to the strike at Coventry they would also be locked out. The union was facing the prospect of supporting 4,500 members.

The Executive Committee was summoned to a Council of War. Its deliberations, interrupted by frequent phone calls to the company representatives, ended with an agreement to have yet another meeting between the union and the management. This took place on 14 October when the strike was thirteen weeks old. The attendance included the full Executive Committee, all the full-time officials who covered Rolls-Royce sites and the representatives of the members from those parts of the combine who were still holding out. At the main Rolls-Royce plant at Derby a local agreement had been reached.

It was a long and stormy meeting lasting well into the evening. In London's Tothill Street, outside the headquarters of the Employers' Federation, hundreds of members were demonstrating, cheering and chanting. At one part of the day one of the Rolls-Royce Personnel Directors put his head out of the third floor window to see what all the noise was about. Instantly he was seen, the whole demonstration as if it had been rehearsed roared in one voice "jump".

The hours of negotiations finally came to an end. The Rolls-Royce management put on the table a final improved offer. The union side looked it over and decided to recommend it to the members. The Coventry members accepted. They had achieved a 12 per cent increase; the original offer of £2.25 per week going up to £4.25. As the Coventry claim was based on comparisons with going rates in the district, the other plants had to settle for a slight improvement on the original 7 per cent. The strings attached to the offer, which the union found so unacceptable, were dropped altogether.

When the dust had settled the Director General of the Employers' Federation admitted publicly that they had used the dispute in an effort to determine a comprehensive wage level in the industry. Helped by the voluntary levy paid by the membership the union was able to meet the £250,000 cost of the lockout.

This was the second time a powerful employers' group had tried to break DATA (the first was the Shipbuilders in 1967). Both failed because they totally misjudged the depth of loyalty the members felt for their union. A photograph in the May 1971 issue of DATA Journal showed a smiling John Jones, Chairman of Coventry Central Branch handing over to the DATA Vice President, Mike Cooley, a cheque for £13,000, the largest donation the union had ever received. It was the result of a collection taken up among the locked out members when they had returned to work.

The post mortem was held at the Annual Conference. The delegates acknowledged that this dispute had caused problems in other parts of the organisation. The weight of support being given to the Rolls-Royce members limited what could be done for those who had disputes in other firms. The Conference congratulated the Coventry members for holding out against the employers' attack but asked the EC to investigate methods for dealing with any future confrontations between DATA and large industrial combines.

In the end the EC, the Divisional Councils and the Branches took a determined stand against extravagant adventurism emanating from ultra-left groups. The lesson had been learned. Realistic assessments of the outcome of disputes would now be a factor in the union's future industrial policy.

on the political stage

Only simpletons such as professional politicians and pollsters claim they know what people are thinking. The reality is that the views of the collective can only be derived from those who care to express them. The politics of a trade union are the politics of an articulate minority. The silent majority who by definition nobody hears, either accepts or is indifferent to the political stance taken by the organisation. It is an error to assume it is "anti". Determining the union's stand on any issue has been the responsibility of lay members. Its democracy is such that it requires their voluntary participation. Those who choose not to take part in the process are expected to live with the decisions taken. Nobody, so far, has come up with a more practical scheme. A remarkable feature of the Association has been its extraordinarily high proportion of active members: a fact evidenced by its effectiveness at the workforce. The disputes it became engaged in, the gains it achieved, its success in recruitment of new members were the result of active lay member participation. Only with an army of activists in the field could the union have maintained the efficiency of its organisation, administration and communication.

DATA was never reticent or ambivalent when it came to publishing its political position. It was clearly on the left and it used all its channels of communication to try and persuade the membership that was the correct place to be. Members who disagreed had equal access to the same channels. The "Draughtsman" and later "DATA Journal" in its monthly editorial laid down the union's line on the political, economic and social issues of the day.

It invited criticism and comment and it got it. The correspondence columns resounded with broadsides from every part of the political spectrum. Epistolary battles and often duels were fought over a selection of topics which have endured to the present day. Over the years members went on arguing about nationalisation, privatisation, education, nuclear weapons, atomic power, communism, capitalism, fascism, socialism, the USSR, the USA, the EEC. They pursued the solutions of the Irish question. They applied sweet reason, dialectics, logic and downright assertion to the problems of working women, religion, housing, social services, law and order, pornography, racism and the uses of technology. And never absent for long were the voices which insisted a union should just be a union and have nothing to do with politics of any shade.

Delegates to the 1944 Annual Conference agreed that the membership should be balloted on the question of political action and that a committee should be elected to campaign for the establishment of a political fund. Conference had also decided that if the vote was in favour the Association would affiliate to the Labour Party. The vote in favour was overwhelming. Association members had taken the first step towards having a voice in Parliament.

In the 1959 General Election, Mr J Jarvie and Mr E Mackenzie, who stood as AESD sponsored candidates for Cathcart (Glasgow) and Wembley South, respectively, failed to defeat their Conservative opponents. Things improved in the 1964 election. Three DATA members became MPs: Mr E S Bishop for Newark, Mr W Howie for Luton and Mr R L Howarth for Bolton East. Mr A E Booth who stood for Tynemouth was narrowly defeated by Dame Irene Ward (Conservative). Messrs Bishop and Booth were officially sponsored by the union.

In 1966 when Harold Wilson asked for a better majority all four were successful, A E Booth winning the Barrow-in-Furness seat. The Editorial in the July 1970 issue of DATA Journal opened with "Wilson has lost. Having presented the electorate with a presidential choice it did not choose him." That said it all. Nevertheless, DATA retained three sponsored MPs with Mr J Ashton winning the seat at Bassetlaw and joining Messrs Bishop and Booth on the Labour benches.

When Edward Heath in 1974 decided it was his turn to pose the question, who rules, the answer was - the Labour Party. DATA by this time had become Technical, Administrative and Supervisory Section of the Amalgamated Union of Engineering Workers (TASS) and had now four sponsored MPs. J A Lamond won Oldham East and lined up with the winning team of Bishop, Booth and Ashton. As far as the union was concerned the icing on the parliamentary cake was the appointment of Albert Booth as Minister of State for Employment.

Although it never failed to publicise the prowess of its sponsored MPs (Albert Booth got front page treatment in the Journal not only when he became a Minister but also when he spoke against Harold Wilson's incomes policy) DATA's radical reputation was gained from the policies it adopted at Annual Conference and from the statements of representatives at the TUC, the Labour Party and the Confederation of Shipbuilding and Engineering Unions.

The basic premise behind the union's political thinking was that statutory interference in the relationship between an organised workforce and its employer was unnecessary. In other words a union and an employer should be free to negotiate their way to a mutually acceptable bargain on pay and conditions of employment. DATA acted in the belief that this was the logical procedure in a capitalist economy where labour was a commodity to be bought and sold in the market place.

The critical event which swung the Association's politics to the left was the winning at the 1943 Annual Conference of the decision to go for a national agreement on minimum rates rather than simply advising members not to take jobs at firms which did not pay them. From that time on the EC, which consisted mainly of centre-right inclined, elderly chief draughtsmen, was committed to supporting members who took industrial action over pay claims.

To those who initiated and defended this policy it was axiomatic that industrial action without political understanding was a fruitless exercise, the labour of Sisyphus. Political action was what was needed to turn society in the direction of a planned economy and the resolution of conflicting interests. At the 1959 Annual Conference J E Mortimer, supporting a motion calling on the AESD to intensify its programme of political education at weekend schools, said "if full employment was to be permanent it was essential to extend the area of social ownership. Periodic booms and slumps were inevitable in an economic system in which the greater parts of the industry remained in private hands." DATA clearly went along with the theories of marxist economics.

There was nothing marxist about the rank and file members. Their objectives were essentially short term - a better return for their labour. Be that as it may the left in the Association argued that a union necessarily be less wholehearted and less effective in meeting the short term aspirations of its members if at the same time it agreed with the principles of the capitalist system. From the end of World War II policies underlining the Association's attachment to the left-wing of the Labour Movement flowed from the Annual Conference of the Representative Council. There were never any signs of serious complaints from the rank and file.

The high level of political consciousness of the activists was persistently demonstrated by the range and nature of the policies behind which the Association threw its support. As far back as the late fifties and early sixties the Association in line with the policies carried at its own Annual Conference, supported the radical wings of the TUC and the Labour Party. In the great debate which took place at the Labour Party Annual Conference in 1960 DATA voted with the majority in favour of unilateral nuclear disarmament and with the minority on the question of getting out of NATO. In 1961 in a similar debate the Party altered its position on unilateral disarmament. The DATA delegates this time were with the minority. That year George Cornes, the union's Nottingham based organiser, made an effective statement opposing Britain's application to join the European Economic Community but the Party decided to hedge its bets on that issue.

More often than not the contributions by Association delegates to the Labour Party and TUC Conference were a trifle too explicit for institutions which described themselves as "broad churches". In the sixties DATA attributed Britain's economic problems to the sharp rise in the cost of raw materials, high interest rates, excessive military spending and the refusal of the engineering employers to pay draughtsmen and allied technicians enough. What it prescribed was the nationalisation of the means of production, distribution and exchange. In practical terms DATA reserved its most determined political challenge to attempts by any Government to interfere with collective bargaining procedures or to impose statutory restrictions on trade union activity. The House of Lords judgment in the Rookes-Barnard case compelled DATA to bring to the 1964 TUC and Labour Party Conference a motion demanding legislative changes which would ensure trade unions the protection they believed the 1906 Trades Disputes Act intended. On this issue both bodies gave their full support.

Without reservation the Association acknowledged Labour to be the mass party of the British working class and the TUC as the unique voice of the national trade union movement. It saw the interaction between these institutions as the only plausible agency for bringing about a committed socialist administration. Its Annual Conference delegates gave short shrift to speakers from the extreme left and the right who, from time to time, tried to persuade them to vote in favour of disaffiliation from the Labour Party. One claimed it was too right wing, the other it was too far to the left.

Nonetheless, there were clear signs that Harold Wilson's Government was inclined to lump trade unionists in with all the other causes of the country's economic troubles. And while the media was equivocal in support of Labour policies at any time, it was enthusiastically backing government criticisms of the trade union movement. Headlines and editorials were well larded with words like "wildcat", "go slow", "work to rule", "closed shop". The British media always had a weakness for easy targets. In the meantime interested parties had made submissions to the Royal Commission on Trade Unions and Employer Associations which the Government had set up under the chairmanship of Lord Donovan in 1964. The main thrust of DATA's submission was that industrial relations would improve if both sides of industry knew where they stood and were represented by well-organised bodies which would command the respect of their constituents.

The Donovan Report came out in 1968 and immediately DATA was up in arms. The report seemed to contain everything the Association was against. "It seeks to limit the rights of trade unionists, particularly at shopfloor and office level" said the Executive Committee. "And" it went on, "it is closely tied to the operations of an incomes policy". There was a general uneasiness among most of the unions over some of the implications of the Report's recommendations. DATA was one of the fist of those demanding a re-call of the TUC Conference. To make sure there were no doubts about where it stood DATA published and circulated throughout the movement a pamphlet entitled "Donovan Exposed".

The TUC response was to arrange a series of "Post Donovan" conferences. The representatives of unions in different industrial sectors were to get together, discuss the Donovan Report and decide what they were going to do about it. DATA representatives were at the meetings of the engineering, shipbuilding and non-manual workers in the private industry group. While all this was going on the TUC found itself facing Barbara Castle's recipe for industrial peace, "In Place of Strife". Donovan faded into the background.

With clinical precision DATA dissected this White Paper, analysed its proposals and came to the conclusion that it was aimed at drastically reducing the strength of trade union organisation. As a follow up to 'Donovan Exposed' it published and circulated its criticisms throughout the movement. It further urged individual members, branches and divisional councils to write to the newspapers and their MPs, to send protest motions to trades councils and Labour Party branches, to raise the subject with shop stewards and to take part in protest demonstrations. The DATA MPs, Albert Booth and Joe Ashton were briefed to make the union's protest in the House. Once again DATA was among the unions calling for the TUC Conference to be reconvened.

In the end the agitation seemed to pay off. The Government withdrew the penal clauses from the White Paper and adopted proposals in the TUC's alternative "Programme for Action" with a view to further discussions on a new Industrial Relations Bill (1970).

DATA was sceptical about this apparently successful demonstration of trade union pressure. There was a general election coming up and the Tories had made it clear that if they won, legislation to control the unions would be a priority issue. "This" said the EC "would result in an even more serious situation". How right it was.

It was not long after the Tories, under Edward Heath, were swept into power that the plans for curbing trade union activity were published. The editorial in the November 1970 issue of DATA Journal almost, but not quite, said, come back "In Place of Strife" all is forgiven. "In Place of Strife" it said "had a group of obnoxious clauses which would have restricted hard-won liberties. This docu-

LOBBY FOR JOBS... 1967 campaign brings representatives of the North East to Downing Street.

ment is so restrictive that it is hard to place it in its historical resting place. Certainly its home is not in the 20th century". DATA wanted an all out campaign against what it called "the destruction of civilised industrial relations and free collective bargaining".

Reborn on 1 January 1971 as the Technical Administrative and Supervisory Section of the Amalgamated Union of Engineering Workers, the union launched itself with messianic fervour into the campaign to kill the Tory Industrial Relations Bill. Its communications system between Head Office and members in the workplaces, in the branches and in the regional groups vibrated with the flow of information, warnings, exhortations and appeals urging every member to come out on the marches and stoppages which were organised to demonstrate the solidarity of the official trade union movement's opposition to the proposed legislation.

Encouraged by active members and taking to heart the advice from the EC that they should co-operate with shopfloor and other staff unions TASS members in general rallied to the cause. The union banners were seen at the protest rallies, the one-day stoppages and especially at the mammoth "Kill the Bill" demonstration in Trafalgar Square on Sunday 21

February 1971. To those who argued that the protests would not prevent the Bill becoming law and that the time for taking action was when that happened, George Doughty, in an article in Tribune, replied "those who will not oppose its introduction may find reasons for not taking action to defend workers who fall victim to its clauses."

Although it was less confident about the impact of its overall membership, TASS through its leadership and activists, continued to articulate the industrial and political arguments for total opposition to the legislation. Along with Hugh Scanlon of the Engineering Union and Jack Jones of the Transport and General Workers Union they brought a formidable influence to bear on a rather unheroic TUC.

It was obvious that certain prominent members of the General Council of the TUC were not enthusiastic about the idea of a vigorous challenge to the Government. Under the proposed legislation unions would have to register. At a special Conference held in March at Croydon a rather loosely-worded recommendation on the question of whether or not unions ought to register allowed some union leaders to state that they were prepared to carry out that part of the law. A motion instructing unions "not to register under the Industrial Relations Act and to take measures to remove themselves from the provisional register" was successfully moved by Hugh Scanlon at the 1971 Congress. "Not one union must register" he declared. "A single scratch can lead to gangrene". George Doughty replied to those delegates who were claiming they would have to register in order to protect themselves from being encroached by staff associations and so-called professional bodies. "If anyone believes they can remain registered and continue opposition to the Act through non-compliance with all or even some of its other provisions, they are grossly deceiving themselves" he warned.

TASS's widespread lobbying and its alliance with powerful shop floor organisations like the Engineers, the Boilermakers and the Transport and General Workers had undoubtedly been a significant factor in ensuring that the TUC was not going to compromise with the Tory trade union legislation.

On 5 August 1971 the Industrial Relations Act received royal assent. The heavy hand of the law was now poised over the British trade unions. At first everyone appeared to be looking the other way, either through embarrassment or just waiting to see who was going to make the first move. DATA summoned a one- day recall of its Representative Council where the delegates gave unanimous approval for the formal removal of the union's name from the Registrar General's roll. In a statement to the delegates the Executive Committee warned that the decision to de-register "will involve the risk that substantial compensation may be awarded against the union and its officials resulting in a considerable weakening of the union's financial position." Fortunately this fear did not materalise, which was just as well as the funds were under some strain from having to meet an increasing number of claims for unemployment benefit.

It was the Transport and General Workers Union and the AUEW, Engineering Section, which bore the brunt of the National Industrial Relations Court's onslaught. These were the unions which contributed most to the trade union folklore of the early seventies: the dockers, the Pentonville Five, the Official Solicitor, Goad, Con Mech and the word "sequestration".

In November 1972 the Government decided to shore up its industrial relations laws with a wage freeze. TASS instantly reacted with another publication detailing once again its arguments against interference in free collective bargaining and for good measure reminding the General Council of the TUC that incomes policies never provided answers to Britain's economic problems.

The TUC recalled Congress on 5 March 1973 to discuss the consequences of the wage freeze. The announcement by the Congress Standing Orders Committee that there should be no motions or amendments to the TUC policy document gave some idea of how the General Council intended to play this issue. It did not get far. A reference back of the Standing Orders recommendation was successful. The General Council thought again and agreed to accept motions and amendments.

Harry Urwin of the TGWU moved and George Doughty, on behalf of the whole AUEW, seconded a resolution calling on the TUC "to organise and lead co- ordinated action in support of affiliated unions in dispute and who require such support. And also, "to invite affiliated unions to join in a day of national protest and stoppage against wage freeze policy and increases in food prices; this to be organised as quickly as possible." Despite the rather pedestrian prose the message was clear. The General Council called for the stoppage on the most appropriate day, 1 May. Millions of trade unionists all over the country took part. The reports reaching the EC showed that throughout the divisions the great majority of members took the day off and demonstrated alongside members of other trade unions.

Throughout the chequered lifespan of the Industrial Relations Act the Association, which by that time had become a white collar section of the AUEW, persisted in discharging its policy obligations. In the words of the Executive Committee "it was business as usual." The phases of the Government's wage freeze were as much honoured in the breach as they were in the observance. Office representatives met no resistance to the inclusion of "not legally binding" clauses in agreements. Many employers were giving undertakings to lay aside increases to be paid out when the Government position changed. In the majority of large engineering firms members were acknowledging their alliance with the shopfloor workers by taking part in shop stewards' meetings. Mutual support in dispute situations was now the rule rather than the exception. In spite of the restrictions of the legal system the union was growing and flourishing. Signs of this progress could be seen from the Association's performance at the Trade Union Congress and to a slightly less extent at the Labour Party's Annual Conference.

From the time it had become DATA the Association more often than not had great difficulty in finding support for its policies at the TUC and Labour Party Conference. Its opposition to incomes policy was well known and often heard but was nearly always at odds with TUC and Labour party conventional opinion. How DATA fared in dealing with broad economic questions depended on whether the Labour Party was in government or in opposition. J E Mortimer's speech against joining the Common Market won resounding applause at the 1962 Congress but lost the vote against the General Council's wait and see policy.

When the very much more domestic issue of the expulsion of the ETU from Congress came up in 1961 the DATA delegates voted against the General Council recommendation. There was no way DATA would ever condone the ballot rigging which took place in the election for the post of General Secretary of the ETU. Nonetheless, neither would DATA accept that the TUC should make 250,000 members of one of the important industrial unions suffer for the fraudulent practice of five officials. The General Council was adamant and the delegates voted overwhelmingly for the ETU to be disaffiliated. The Labour Party Conference took the same view as the TUC and the ETU was expelled from the Party. Once again DATA voted with the minority.

But as the sixties progressed DATA's influence began to take effect. At the 1967 Brighton Congress it was among the unions which defeated the General Council with a motion sharply critical of the Labour Government's economic policies. Success also came in the carrying of a resolution, in the name of DATA and the Boilermakers Society, condemning the Prices and Incomes Acts. DATA's continually repeated view that the British Government should disassociate itself from the US policy in Vietnam also won the approval of Congress. Had it not been for an oversight in dealing with the nominating papers George Doughty would almost certainly have been elected to the General Council. At the Labour Party Conference later in the year the party hierarchy was forced to pull out all the stops to defeat the DATA motion against taking the UK into the Common Market.

The 1968 Trades Union Congress, started badly for DATA. News came through that one of its delegates, Jim Cowie, a Scottish activist had gone missing in a boating accident. It was later confirmed that he had drowned.

When the big economic debate got under way powerful speeches from Hugh Scanlon, Frank Cousins and George Doughty saw off the opposition to a motion rejecting any legislation which would hinder legitimate trade union activity in seeking improvements in wage and salary levels. To cap what was a very successful week George Doughty was elected with an overwhelming majority to the new Technical Engineering and Scientific Section of the General Council. With Hugh Scanlon, Jack Jones of the TGWU and several other progressives on the Council DATA saw the opportunity of moving the TUC much further towards the left.Such movement was less evident at the Labour Party Conference. The NEC defended the government's policies sometimes rather desperately. A resolution from a Liverpool constituency party which criticised the economic policy of the government was rejected by the barest majority. There was nothing the NEC could do to prevent the majority throwing out the idea of a statutory incomes policy. This at least pleased the DATA delegation.

DATA's and subsequently TASS's uncompromising opposition to any form of interference with the union's freedom to determine its own rules and to use its bargaining power as it wished was based on understanding the realities of the world of industry. Like raw materials and other services labour was a cost that the employer had to meet. Its value fluctuated with market conditions, scarce labour was expensive and unskilled labour cheap. The economic advantage in meeting these costs had to be with the employer. The human factor in the marketing of labour allowed the necessity of commercial advantage to be translated into a determinant of social status. The employers of labour claimed and imposed superior rights. The disadvantages for the individual employee were stark. The outcome was the formation of trade unions. Acting collectively the employees could go some way towards redressing the imbalance in their relationship with the employers.

Constraints on trade union organisation and activity from whatever source tilted the balance in favour of the employer. It was illogical for a union not to oppose such constraints while at the same time claiming it offered its members a means of protecting and improving their conditions of employment. Draughtsmen were nothing if not logical.

the broad left, the right and the ultra left

Within a capitalist economy it is widely held that an industrial workforce should co-operate whole-heartedly with judgments and decisions made by or on behalf of a company's directors. Those who think otherwise are pejoratively labelled militants or communists or communist dominated. The founding fathers of the AESD would have been horrified at the very idea of such labels being applied to them. Nonetheless they never doubted that the interests of their members and of those who employed them were in opposition. It was the discovery of this fact which led them to form their organisation in the first place and to the conclusion that co-operation with the employers could only be on the terms of negotiated agreements. As its membership grew and extended over a broader range of occupations the Association absorbed fresh industrial experiences and further refined its level of political consciousness. But it also brought a reaction both from craft centred traditionalists who resented change and expansion and from those who kept faith with the capitalist system.

There was a period during the forties when the Executive Committee was dominated by a group whose leanings were, in political terms, to the right of centre. They envisaged the Association as an exclusive, professional society with a membership restricted to those who might impress the employers with their technical prestige. United in their opposition to anything that seemed to come from the left, their aim was for the Association to defer to the official line of the Labour Party and the TUC. This meant ignoring progressive policies.

Left wing activists were convincing the membership of the need for a more militant stand to defend their living standards. It was being made clear that continued control by the so-called moderates would result in a thriving union becoming a diminutive, harmless navel-contemplating industrial sect: something that would be approved by the engineering employers and the British media.

Once it was discovered that the centre-right traditionalists were circulating voting lists to get their men to influential committees and conference delegations and at the same time naming those they wanted to keep off them, irrespective of their potential persuasion, the left set about creating a counter organisation.

There is a media-created myth that the left gains power in trade unions through the apathy of the general membership. The opposite is more likely to be true. Keeping the members in the dark and hoping that not too many questions would be asked was the tactic of those who wanted the Association to back away from confrontations with employers and to restrict recruitment to time-served draughtsmen. Left-wing activists began to campaign patiently and widely among rank and file members. In the offices, at the branches and divisional councils they raised issues and explained measures that would give the Association a much more energetic thrust in dealing with their problems. Attitudes changed, more members began to get involved, left candidates won the support they needed to be elected to leadership positions. The Association was transformed. It was clearly evident that without the widespread support of the rank and file members the broad left breakthrough could not have taken place.

From the 1950s onwards the Association was confirmed in its progressive course. The membership grew. Its appetite for militant action increased and in the wider labour movement its delegates argued with notable conviction for a more radical stance on social, economic and political issues.

DATA was like the gadfly of Socrates. It buzzed around the TUC and Labour Party Conferences stinging the comfortable, the complaisant and the cowardly. It was on the side of those who opposed Hugh Gaitskell's defence policy in 1960. It was against Britain's membership of NATO.

It backed the Ban-The- Bomb Campaign and it spoke out against the US missile bases on British soil. It called for closer co-operation with the countries of Eastern Europe. It deplored the US intervention in Cuba and Vietnam in 1961. It called for support for the Civil Rights Movement. The fate of Dave Kitson added emphasis to its support for the Anti-Apartheid Movement. In the 1975 Common Market referendum, as TASS, it was deeply involved in the campaign for a "No" vote.

The Trade Union and Labour Party delegates who year after year packed the seaside conference halls were never in doubt about where DATA and TASS stood on the major political and industrial topics.

Other white collar unions in the public and private sectors had from time to time aligned themselves with the left of the movement. But not with the consistency of DATA and TASS. A problem for some of these organisations was their failure to handle the ideas and policies promulgated by Trotskyist groups.Ultra-leftism was espoused by a tiny minority found among activist in the trade union and labour movement. They were more commonly members of white collar unions. The down-to-earth nature of the shopfloor organisations offered little encouragement to revolutionary theorising. The perceived status superiority associated with white collar occupation may have been responsible for temperaments that felt the need to be in the field of conjectural politics. The political experience they may have acquired usually came from excursions in the Labour and Communist Parties. Their defection was mainly due to impatience with what they believed were gradualist approaches towards socialist ends. Prominent among the Association's ultra-left were supporters of the Maoist theories on the construction of socialism that had gained currency among a few ultra-left intellectuals during the late sixties and the early seventies. They got very little sympathy in the broad left. They did find allies amongst some of the small Trotskyist groups that were always around and with them tried to direct the leftward drift in the union towards more extravagant revolutionary positions.

The tactic used by this group was to move Resolutions at Annual Conference which if passed would commit the Executive Committee to supporting any kind of industrial action. The broad left responded by lining up speakers to enter the debates and expose how the principle of accountability was being disregarded. When their Resolutions failed the ultra-left would blame the leadership. The right wing, on the other hand, was never the main target for ultra-left criticism. Instead they concentrated their attacks on the alliance of Labour and Communist Party members whose policies and status in the councils of the union they resented.

There were occasions when the Conference delegates were treated to the spectacle of the ultra-left and known right wingers voting together against the broad left. Only one full-time official ever revealed that he had ultra-left leanings. At a critical stage in a difficult dispute he declared that he would rather see the union destroyed than compromise with an employer: an exotic disposition peculiar to certain Japanese airmen.

Much has been written and said about the role of the Communist Party in the British trade union movement. There is a generally held assumption that all Communists thought and acted in exactly the same manner irrespective of the industrial environment they inhabited; they were, it was thought, compelled to toe the party line. The fact that they were as likely to be as varied and as prejudiced in their outlook as any other collection of trade unionists always seemed to be overlooked. Communists were not immune from the experience they acquired as white collar, blue collar, public or private sector workers.

Draughtsmen as has already been noted had a penchant for accurate observation and attention to detail. These were characteristics that pervaded their union activity. While it is true that Communist draughtsmen may have had a more distinct political perspective than their colleagues they were never that much different in their craft-centred approach of finding appropriate solutions to given problems. The records of the proceedings of Annual Conferences carry evidence of the number of times Communist Party members were on opposite sides in important debates. The "broad" in broad left had more to do with principles than with details. They understood that a trade union could not play the role of a political party. Its function was to organise workers so that they could protect and advance their conditions of employment. Politics came into it when the state or its agencies took steps to limit or prevent unions from carrying out their objectives.

The media reference to the Communist-led Draughtsmen's Union was intended to misrepresent the purpose of a successful organisation that served technologists and technicians working in a vital sector of the national economy. Unlike his predecessor, who was at no time referred to as "Labour Party member" George Doughty, the General Secretary from 1975 had to be "Communist" Ken Gill. The rate at which the union was growing showed that technical staff was more impressed by the industrial relations experience, effective organisation and a leadership that got results than by the insinuation that they were being manipulated in some sort of industrial conspiracy.

Irrespective of their political inclination every activist and full-time official was under a strict obligation to carry out and defend the policies determined by lay members at the union's Annual Conference. That commitment and the participation of the membership contributed to the union's reputation and its success.

the AUEW amalgamation

As early as 1919 when the Association was only six years old amalgamation was being seriously discussed. The question came up as a result of an invitation from the Amalgamated Society of Engineers offering draughtsmen an autonomous section within its structure.

A few leading members were eager to pursue the issue. These included the Editor of The Draughtsman, George Thomson, who saw amalgamation as a step towards bringing draughtsmen into closer involvement with the wider trade union movement. The Executive Committee were less enthusiastic fearing the advantages of a small tightly organised craft-based union would eventually disappear in the large organisation. The discussions came to nothing.

In 1925 the question came up again. A delegate from Coventry stated at the Annual Conference that what was needed was a single industrial union for all workers in the engineering industry. The delegates liked it. The Executive Committee agreed to set up a working party to look into the possibilities and report back the following year. As was their wont the draughtsmen did the job carefully and in detail.

In practical terms it was a fruitless exercise. The report did, however, reveal the enormous weaknesses of the trade union organisation in the engineering and shipbuilding industry. It was difficult enough according to the report to get the fifty separate unions in the industry, each with its own sectional interest, its own benefits and its own deeply held traditions to communicate, never mind amalgamate.

Another invitation was received in 1927. This time the Foundry Workers were suggesting that the unions in the industry ought to get together and have another go at the amalgamation problem. After a debate over whether or not they should accept the Draughtsmen replied, in somewhat frosty tones, they did not think the time was opportune for the AESD to amalgamate with other unions.

This ought to have killed the notion of amalgamation stone dead. But no. The progressives on both sides were keeping it alive. During 1943, 1944 and 1945 AESD representatives were talking once again to the AEU. The Executive Committee was far from enthusiastic about "one big union" but it was persuaded to consult the branches and to have the issue placed on the agenda of the 1946 Annual Conference. Conference came to an end before the item was reached.

Up until 1958 nothing was being done officially about amalgamation. Then at the Annual Conference a resolution from Coventry West Branch said that other engineering unions should be approached in a genuine effort to seek amalgamation and thereby strengthen the co-operation between staff and manual workers. The Executive Committee took this on board and contacted the Association of Supervisory Staffs, Executives and Technicians, the Association of Scientific Workers and the Amalgamated Engineering Union. These three unions replied cautiously, saying they would be in favour of exploratory talks. Initially the two white collar unions seemed anxious to get as far as they could with these discussions but each side knew there were serious difficulties to be overcome. The Executive Council of the Engineering Union was very interested in advancing co-operation and entered into the talks with enthusiasm.

By 1962 all parties had reached the stage of agreeing to set up joint committees to see where they could co-operate. The meetings with ASSET were few and far between and in the case of the AEU they were having difficulties getting off the ground. A motion at the 1962 Annual Conference of what was now DATA, from Newcastle West Branch, which tried to scupper the whole idea of amalgamation, failed to get the two-thirds majority in favour of it being discussed. And so the search for the magic formula that would bring all the unions into one fold went on.

In March 1963 a set of proposals emerged from the AEU. The plan was that over a five year period the unions' committees would liaise at branch, district and national levels. There would be an exchange of non-voting representatives at each other's policy making conferences. During the five years they would establish a National Engineering Federation made up of representatives from the unions involved. Its purpose would be to discuss general questions. It would not issue instructions. A general working party would be in session to see if, after the first five years, closer co-operation would be possible, say in relation to certain services, contributions and benefits. DATA responded positively and further suggested the mutual exchange of representatives at weekend schools where the relationship between the two unions could be discussed.

While all this was going on the ASCW had approached ASSET for what it claimed were talks about setting up a federation of technical unions. As far as DATA was concerned such a body would be no different from the already existing Joint Consultative Committee of Staff Unions which met under the auspices of the Confederation of Engineering and Shipbuilding Unions.

In his fraternal address to the 1964 Annual Conference Mr (later Sir) John Boyd, Executive Council Member of the AEU made a number of significant comments. John Boyd's style was half-joking, half serious and the odd throw-away line. He was, in fact, an extremely subtle and shrewd communicator. "Being a sort of political animal myself" he told Conference with folksy relish, "the three main qualities in getting to the top in any political party were, instability, unreliability and airy-fairness". In his opinion the people least qualified to criticise trade unions were politicians. "Frequently they never had a rule book in their hands at all and did not know what they were talking about". It was, he said, the politicians who were complaining about too many unions in British industry and advising more amalgamations. John Boyd was cool on these suggestions. He warned about the power of an industrial union with the wrong policies. "It might bring the industry to its knees, on the other hand it could commit hara-kiri in the process." "It was wise" he went on, "to have a number of different unions looking after the special interests of different craftsmen and different classes of workers and technicians". What he foresaw was a "strong and established federation .. whereby DATA would always remain DATA and the AEU would always be the AEU." The President of DATA thanked John Boyd for his address which he said was "very much appreciated". It was not recorded whether or not the delegates appreciated they had been listening to an Executive Officer of the second largest industrial union in the country and one which was anxiously pursuing as many small craft unions as it could in order to absorb them into its own structure.

Anyway, the statements emerging from successive Annual Conferences during the sixties showed DATA was becoming more and more committed to the idea of one union for the engineering industry. Report followed report on the progress being made at branch and district level on the liaison taking place between DATA and AEU members. But nothing seemed to be happening at national level. At the 1967 Conference, when DATA was in the throes of the shipbuilding lockout, delegates took the opportunity of coming to the rostrum to publicise the support they were getting from the AEU members in the shipbuilding industry. There was also a very welcome donation of £2,000 from the EC of the AEU towards the dispute fund. Said J E Mortimer, "whatever our long term perspectives may be on amalgamation there is no doubt at all that the interests of our members will be served by developing the closest possible unity with other engineering workers."

Scarborough 1968 and the fraternal address to the DATA Conference was given by Hugh Scanlon, the newly-elected President of what was now the Amalgamated Union of Engineering and Foundry Workers (the AEF). Scanlon did not mince words. "The AEF was sincerely looking forward to the working out of mutually acceptable arrangements for amalgamation with DATA. Both unions were viable and progressive." Things were starting to move. The talk was no longer about "if we" or "should we", but "when we".

Technological developments in industry, the resulting increase and diversity in technician staff, the interest of other unions in this market for members, the diminishing number of draughtsmen and the cost of supporting long-running strikes, were the principal factors prompting DATA's progress towards the AEF. An editorial comment in the November 1969 issue of the DATA Journal said "We must be part of an organisation who if we repulse them will, in any case, recruit these technicans."

To reassure the large number of members who still harboured doubts about the outcome of a marriage between, in their view, a rather elite workforce and manual workers, the DATA Executive Committee kept emphasising it did not intend in any way to sacrifice the Association's identity or independence. In the June 1969 issue of the DATA Journal the editorial spelt this out:

"A defensive merger is in our interests provided always that our identity remains. With that identity and the characteristics which we have developed, strengthened by the link with the AEF, such a coalition would ensure the most powerful staff union in Britain."

It was a pitch aimed at the militants who wanted a bigger army and at those who just wanted a union that was more likely to deliver the improvements in pay.

As the talks progressed the conditions DATA required before it would put the matter to the vote of the members were expressed in ten points: **1.** That there shall be within the engineering union a permanent place for the "TECHNICIANS GROUP" and this group will have its own title; **2.** That the GROUP shall have its own rules; **3.** That the GROUP shall have its own subscriptions and benefits; **4.** That the

MOVING TOGETHER... Industrial co-operation between the AEF and DATA heralded the eventual amalgamation the two organisations.

GROUP will be responsible for the election of its own full-time and lay member officials; **5.** That the GROUP shall continue to provide its own services, and publications - including technical publications; **6.** That the GROUP shall have its own branches and divisional councils and executive committee; **7.** That the GROUP will continue its own affiliations to national and international organisations; **8.** That the GROUP will have authority to deal with its own industrial policy, including the right to call strikes of its members. It will not expect the main organisation to pay for this in any way; **9.** That on main national issues the GROUP will accept policies decided by democratic discussions within the engineering union; **10.** The GROUP will make a per capita contribution to central funds to pay for common activities.

Agreement on these conditions meant that the amalgamation was going to start life bearing a close resemblance to what John Boyd envisaged in 1964: a federation whereby DATA remained DATA and the AEF remained the AEF.

In his opening address to the 1970 Annual Conference, Ken Banks, the first President of DATA from Northern Ireland, announced that "the AEF has accepted the principle of autonomy and true to the tradition of the pioneers of our union, our members have voted overwhelmingly for unity, the vote being - against amalgamation 14,864 - for amalgamation 44,757."

Needless to say the ground had been well prepared. The ten points were reiterated again and again. They were explained, interpreted and expounded throughout the whole membership. No technical hitch could be tolerated in the historic decision-making procedure. The activists at the firms, in the branches and divisional councils had been mobilised to ensure that every member understood why it was such an important issue. The EC had made a determined effort to guarantee that the voting method would be foolproof - a postal ballot in which every member would be sure of receiving a form and be given ample time to complete it. The voting took place between 23 February and 1 April 1970.

Ken Banks might have been a trifle modest when he told the conference delegates that he had never expected such a massive vote in favour. Nevertheless, he did say "it had been shown that when the issues are put clearly to the members they will come to the correct decision." An appeal to enlightened self-interest rarely goes unanswered.

The members of the other unions involved in the amalgamation had voted just as substantially as DATA to become a section of the Amalgamated Union of Engineering Workers. The Foundry Workers and the Construction Engineers in particular were noted at the time for their progressive leadership. There was no doubt they saw the new organisation as a step towards the establishment of a powerful influence in one of the most formidable industrial sectors. Not only that but also as a force which would bring greater strength of purpose to the whole of the labour movement. Leaving aside the question of whether it was an amalgamation or simple a federation of independent unions, the early years of the AUEW were full of hope, promise and optimism. Something the employers would not disregard.

The foundation of the new union had been laid with appropriate ceremony. The task that lay ahead was to build the superstructure. To begin with the sine qua non of trade unionism, the rule book had to be dealt with. The "Instrument of Amalgamation" a legal document which was required by the Trade Union (Amalgamations etc.)

Act 1964 to set down the terms and conditions of the amalgamation made it clear that the rules covering the whole Amalgamated Union of Engineering Workers, plus the rules of each of its four sections would be observed. Should there happen to be a conflict between the overall rules and one of the section's own rules the section's rules prevail. So in a way no one was giving up anything.

The Management Committee of the new union consisted of the President and seven members of the Engineering Section, two representatives of the Foundry Section, two from the Technical Section and one from the Construction Section. Its policy-making conference had all fifty-two members of the Engineering Section's National Committee, seven representatives of the Foundry Section, seven from the Technical Section and three from the Construction Section. The fact that the Engineering Section had insisted on retaining all of its Executive Council and its complete policy making committee was a clear indication of the direction of its thinking.

The signs were even clearer at the first meeting of the new NEC held in Eastbourne in July 1970. When the question of the AEU Supervisory Branches came up, a matter of some consequence to the Technical and Supervisory Section of the AUEW, it was suggested that this issue could be left aside until the common rule book was produced. Two months after selling the amalgamation to its members on the basis of maintaining its separate identity DATA was now being pressed to accept the AEU Rule Book. It was pretty obvious that at least two of the sections were on different wavelengths. DATA visualised that the amalgamation would be the launching pad for a brand new, never-before-seen industrial union. For the AEU amalgamation meant what it had always meant, the absorption of other groups into its structure.

To be fair, the philosophy of the AEU had been honed and case-hardened in bitter struggles with brutal employers. It was a union with understandable pride in the craft skills of its membership. They had contributed to the spectacular feats of heavy engineering and shipbuilding in war and peace through the second half of the 19th and into the 20th century. It was convinced beyond question that its internal democracy was superior to that found in any other part of the working class movement. It was not going to be easy to dent, never mind dismantle, the armour of tradition which encased AEU thinking. The AEU would never admit that the glory days were coming to an end. Technological innovation was rapidly de-skilling the crafts. The single owner manufacturing plant was being taken over by, or being merged into, combines and corporations where diversification and transnational control was the name of the game. But even more significant was the indisputable evidence that the jobs for blue collar workers were declining as fast as those for white collar staff were flourishing. Any organisation claiming to be a union for engineering workers that did not have a clearly identified and vigorous white collar section would be heading for extinction. For these reasons DATA was determined to fight for the maintenance of the Technical Administrative and Supervisory Section of the AUEW.

Complications were met at every turn as the NEC struggled with the task of composing a rule book acceptable to all four sections. A paper with suggestions on how this might be achieved was prepared by the Foundry Section's General Secretary, W Simpson. In January 1972 a three-day conclave at the Selsdon Park Hotel ended with the announcement that the NEC was going to set up another Rules Sub-Committee. Headed by DATA's General Secretary, G Doughty, who would be seconded for three months, this committee would undertake the job of producing the final draft of the common rule book.

It did not succeed. Instead it went through an exercise that demonstrated the futility of trying to make a blend of four different unions' rule books. All George Doughty's detailed work was set aside and a new document which became known as the Worthing Proposals was submitted for the consideration of each of the sections. The NEC had agreed that if the Worthing Proposals were endorsed by the sections they would provide the basis for the establishment of a single engineering union. The principles set out were: **1.** One Executive Council; **2.** One National Conference; **3.** One Rules Revision Committee; **4.** One Final Appeal Court; **5.** One financial structure; **6.** A common method of election of officials; **7.** A guarantee of the continuance of the four sections under the control of the Executive Council.

Endorsed by all but the Engineering Section's all-powerful National Committee, these proposals arrived back on the NEC's table. The vision of one union for the engineering industry was beginning to become a little blurred.

Having rejected Worthing, albeit narrowly (the voting was 27 against, 24 for, with one absentee) the National Committee expressed its concern at the lack of progress in integrating the four sections. It instructed its Executive Council to publish not later than September 1974 a report on its proposals on how this should be done. Not only that, but it further instructed the EC to "mount a campaign of explanation and information to the committees and branches through the medium of the AUEW Herald." The EC did nothing, possibly because its proposals for integration were the Worthing Proposals and possibly because nobody said what the "campaign of explanation and information" was to be about. The EC decided that all it could do was to go along with the other sections and try Worthing again at the 1975 National Committee. It would be difficult to say whether any change was expected. But change there was. This time the National Committee once again dismissed Worthing, accepted a motion declaring what was wrong with the proposals and only managed to defeat an addendum saying ".... and in view of the stand taken by other sections, National Committee instructs Executive Council to take immediate constructive steps to dissolve the amalgamation." The voting on the addendum was 29 against 22 for. Perhaps in this context the use of the word "constructive" was just too much. Needless to say the other sections were horrified at the number of votes in favour of dissolution.

The objection to Worthing was that the recommended number of representatives from each of the other sections on the new AUEW committees was not in proportion to the strength of their membership. "Totally unbalanced" complained National Committee, "and places the Engineering Section in a most invidious position." Again the other sections were taken by surprise. The principle of proportional representation never seemed to be given much weight on the National Committee itself. One division of 120,000 members was represented by two committee members as was another division with 15,000 members. Anyway, the National Executive Committee of the AUEW was prepared to take a look at this question. Maybe if adjustments were made some progress could be recorded.

Everyone knows what can happen to the best laid plans of mice and men; Worthing offered no exception. Nor could it be denied that somewhere out there in Britain's great industrial heartland there were forces with a special interest in preventing the formation of a strong organisation capable of representing the common interests of both white and blue collar workers. In August 1975 some three years after the Selsdon Park meeting from which Worthing had emerged their journal gave the rank and file members of the Engineering Section their first glimpse of the twice-rejected proposals. The accompanying editorial emphasised the "unhealthy" state of the current four section loose federation and invited the membership to join in the debate to find the conditions for moulding a "strong unified Union."

It took twelve months of hard bargaining and sharp debate to produce a revamped version of the Worthing Proposals. In the end it was unanimously agreed to recommend that the NEC should stay as it was, that the originally proposed policy-making National Conference should be reduced from 300 delegates to 150 and that it rather than the National Committee should elect the Rules Revision Committee. It was further suggested that some of the more technical aspects of the organisation should be left to await the development of the amalgamation.

The representatives of the Technical Administrative and Supervisory Section had consistently argued that insisting on the periodic election of all full-time officials would repel rather than attract other unions which the AUEW may wish to invite into amalgamation talks. Nonetheless, in the interests of the present amalgamation, TASS was prepared to have all its future officials elected by the membership. It would not, however, alter the contracts of employment of its existing officials. They would be allowed to retain their jobs on the conditions they accepted when they were appointed. The NEC agreed to acknowledge this concession. It was also agreed that the four sections would retain their separate identities under the control of the NEC.

Under the heading of Amalgamation the report of the decisions reached at the 1976 meeting of the National Committee said "the National Committee accepts the NEC proposals as submitted to the 1974 National Committee relative to the principle of amalgamation as embodied in the seven principles, with the following exceptions". It then proceeded to offer a further reduction in the size of the national policy-making conference, rejecting the 150 delegates and offering its own 52 plus seven each from the Foundry and Technical Sections with three from the Construction Engineers, making 69 altogether. There was a consequential alteration to the Rules Revision Committee and a proposal to allow a three year transition period for bringing the TASS benefits into line with those of the other amalgamated members. Completely ignoring the NEC's agreement on the position of TASS full-time officials the National Committee declared that all full-time officials were to be elected by ballot and "in relation to TASS a three year transition period would be allowed. Thereafter they will be elected by ballot". The last item was, a common rule book. The National Committee was making it clear that it was having nothing to do with any new-fangled union structures. Amalgamation meant everybody would have to join the AEU.

The foregoing all began when it appeared that the left was in the ascendancy. The burying of Labour's "In Place of Strife", the forcing of the TUC to lead the successful resistance to the Tory's Industrial Relations Act, the public acclaim for the historic Upper Clyde work-in, and the victories gained by the miners in 1972 and 1974 were signs that organised workers were growing in confidence, perhaps overconfidence.

Between the Selsdon Park Hotel meeting and the issuing of the Worthing Proposals the AUEW Engineering Section made a critical alteration to its rules: the election of officials would from now on be by postal ballots. This meant that members would be no longer required to go to their branch meetings to vote or to get involved in discussions about the suitability or otherwise of the candidates for office. It also meant that the tabloid press would be able to exercise its assumed right to give guidance to the members on whom they should or should not vote for to lead their supposedly independent trade union.

The Engineering Section AEU National Committee was usually finely balanced but inclined to the right. Things were not looking too bright for the left wing of the AUEW when one of its staunchest supporters on the National Executive Council, Eddie Marsden, the General Secretary of the Construction Engineers died in 1975. He was succeeded by John Baldwin who had yet to find his feet. W Simpson, the General Secretary of the Foundry Section had become Chairman of the Health and Safety Commission. He was succeeded by the rightwards inclined R Garland. George Doughty retired and Ken Gill, who never attempted to conceal his membership of the Communist Party, become the General Secretary of the Technical, Administrative and Supervisory Section.

The visible differences between TASS and the Engineering Section were overshadowing a much deeper political divide. Future events would show that neither the constitution of representative committees nor the appointment or election of full-time officials would prove to be obstacles to mergers between unions on the same side of the political fence.

The real issue at this time was wage restraint, the key element in the Labour Government's economic policy. TASS, as it always had done, was declaring that unions should have the right to get as much as they could for their members; the Engineering Section wanted to be seen supporting the policies of the Labour Government and Hugh Scanlon did not want his organisation to become a thorn in the sensitive flesh of Harold Wilson.

Nobody knew better than Scanlon the disposition of right and left wingers on the 69-strong National Conference covering all four sections, which was due to meet at the end of May in Scarborough: the combined vote of the left could easily overturn the small majority on his National Committee that had supported wage restraint. So, with a piece of constitutional sleight of hand he ruled that the decision of his National Committee was mandatory on all its 52 members. The left on the National Conference could then be defeated by 52 to 17. As it turned out the motion supporting the Government policy was carried 36 to nothing. The left wingers had refused to take part in a pointless debate and they abstained from voting.

The three smaller sections let it be known that they were profoundly disturbed by the mandating decision. The in-built majority would guarantee that all the policies of the AUEW would be determined by the Engineering Section's National Committee. Whether he made a mistake or not Hugh Scanlon, considered to be a man of the left, succeeded in throwing the AUEW into confusion as well as ensuring its 1.4 million votes for Labour's Incomes Policy.

By 1978 the Executive Council of the Engineering Section introduced a second and revised set of Worthing proposals. Amongst other things this gave TASS three years to bring its method of selecting full-time officials into line with the balloting procedures of the manual sections. It was clear that the Engineering Section was out to force the pace towards a single engineering union. This was probably because it saw other unions finding satisfactory amalgamation partners all round it or because it hoped it could isolate TASS by making it an offer it would have to refuse.

Taking matters into its own hands the Engineering Section called on the other three sections "to agree forthwith to ballot their members on the second Worthing proposals in conformity with the powers vested in Executive Councils by the Trade Union (Amalgamation) Act of 1964 with a view to establishing a new amalgamated union with a single rule book embodying the "Worthing Proposals by a Transfer of Engagements". It also said that it "intended to approach other kindred trade unions to explore with us the possibility of amalgamating under mutually agreed terms." Among the unions listed were the Electrical, Electronic, Telecommunications and Plumbing Union, the Association of Patternmakers and Allied Craftsmen, the National Society of Metal Mechanics, the National Union of Sheetmetal Workers, Coppersmiths, Heating and Domestic Engineers and the Amalgamated Society of Boilermakers, Shipwrights, Blacksmiths and Structural Workers.

TASS representatives knew very well the possibilities that could arise through the use of the 1964 Act. Bringing other unions into the amalgamation under the Worthing Rules was one thing, changing these at some time in the future to accommodate a union such as the EETPU was another. Frank Chapple, the EETPU's General Secretary, had let it be known that he had no interest in a sectionalised union.

The responses to the invitation to "kindred unions" were depressingly unpromising. The only one that gave what could be interpreted as a positive "maybe" was the EETPU. The most unkindest cut came when the Boilermakers' Society, a union with its roots deep in the shipbuilding and engineering industry voted to amalgamate with the General and Municipal Workers' Union.

With the end of its tether beginning to show the Engineering Section declared that it was going ahead with a ballot of the three manual sections on a recommendation to implement Worthing 2 (revised) and if TASS did not take part then that would be the end of the amalgamation. TASS drew attention to the Rules of the AUEW and pointed out that the amalgamation could only be terminated by a decision of 90 per cent of its National Conference. Unimpressed, the Engineering Section tendered its proposals to the Certification Officer who, to its chagrin, upheld the TASS point of view.

Then, rather unadvisedly, the Engineering Section decided to challenge the Certification Officer's ruling in court. The TASS Executive Committee, ever chary about getting involved with the law, was forced to the conclusion that in their situation the union should enjoin with Certification Officer in the defence of his and its own position. This was, however, a principled decision that the EC was not prepared to implement without consulting the TASS democracy. On 11 October 1980 for only the third time in its history the union summoned the delegates to a recall of the Representative Council. (The first time was when the Editor, J E Mortimer resigned in 1968 and the second was in 1971 when the union declared its stand against the Industrial Relations Act). The implications of the proposed merger of the manual sections were explained to the delegates. There was some concern expressed about the effect of the two sections of the AUEW being on opposite sides in a court hearing but it was agreed without dissent that the rules of the organisation had to be defended. The EC decision was endorsed.

The Court found against the Engineering

Section. For better or worse the AUEW had to remain at it was originally constituted.

Almost without anyone noticing a significant amalgamation did take place. In October 1981 the small but highly skilled workforce in the National Union of Gold, Silver and Allied Trades transferred its engagements to TASS. The significance, lost on the Engineering Section, lay in the fact that a TUC affiliate organising non- white collar craft workers was happy to join the white collar section of the AUEW. TASS had offered NUGSAT industrial autonomy, the right to do its own thing while at the same time playing a part in the processes of the whole union. Conditions that were in complete contrast to the specific demands the Engineering Section was making of prospective clients.

No ideological confrontation is complete without its ironies. From day one of the original amalgamation ballot and right through the unhappy piece TASS and Engineering Section rank and file members down in the plants were busy establishing their closest ever working ties. In virtually every engineering company throughout the country they were automatically recognising each other as members of the same union. TASS office committee representatives were playing an important and welcome role on shop stewards' committees. The policy of the union was to encourage members to support shopfloor industrial action even to the point of coming out on strike with them. The problem of the differing levels of strike pay was dealt with by the TASS Executive Committee stating that its members would receive the same strike pay as the Engineering Section members they were supporting. Certain groups of members were naturally unhappy with this advice but the majority were shrewd enough to recognise the quid pro quo advantages of taking it. At the same time it was not always necessary for TASS members to join the picket lines. Very often it was mutually agreed that they would remain at work and contribute a levy to the shopfloor strike fund.

Throughout the country local full-time officials of the four sections were, where practical, sharing office accommodation. Co-operation was proceeding between Engineering Section District Committees and TASS Divisional Councils, between representatives of all sections on trades councils and on the CSEU District Committees. Members of all sections were taking part in each other's weekend schools. The TASS week-long summer school at Ruskin College, Oxford, always provided a quota of places for members of the other sections. It would have been difficult to find evidence that the constitution of the National Committee or the TASS method of selecting full-time officials were bones of contention with anyone other than the Engineering Section leaders.

If trade union amalgamations were sometimes described in terms of marriage this one was evidently heading for the rocks. Hopes of rapprochement were not helped when Engineering Section General Secretary, Gavin Laird, accused TASS of conducting an adulterous affair with the National Union of Sheet Metal Workers. Ken Gill responded by suggesting perhaps a menage a trois, an arrangement that was offensive to the Engineering Section's Calvinistic ethos. Reconciliation seemed to be out of the question but so was divorce. The court had declared that what the Certification Officer had joined together could not be put asunder unless by mutual consent. The Engineering Section was powerless in a situation that had nothing to its liking. TASS on the other hand continued to give the impression that it was anxious to find a formula that would make the AUEW work.

After consulting with their EC, Ken Gill and

Deputy General Secretary Eric Winterbottom put out a cautious feeler to Gavin Laird suggesting the reconstruction of the AUEW on the basis of two instead of four sections. The idea would certainly relieve the growing problems of the Foundry and Construction Engineering Workers. In the background, much to the consternation of the Engineering Section, TASS was emerging as firm favourite in the Sheet Metal Workers' quest for amalgamation; a situation fraught with interesting possibilities.

Talks began on the changes that would have to be made to the AUEW rules. This was an exercise that would take some time as it involved extensive consultations with the legal advisors of both sides. In the meantime the members of the National Union of Sheet Metal Workers, Coppersmiths, Heating and Domestic Engineers had voted overwhelmingly to amalgamate with TASS; a decision that did nothing for TASS/Engineering Section relations. And when TASS announced that George Guy, the ex-Sheet Metal Workers' General Secretary was now General Secretary of the TASS "Craft Section" Gavin Laird accused Ken Gill of setting up a rival union to poach his members. In his reply to the charge Ken Gill said "he would have thought that the Engineering Section would have welcomed the success of our section with mergers since overall it increases the influence and effectiveness of the AUEW". Gavin Laird was not amused.

Relationships within the AUEW had now reached the stage where Terry Duffy, the Engineering Section President, was making no secret of his wish to get rid of TASS. He was now concentrating all his attention on Frank Chapple's EETPU, a kindred organisation that shared his distaste of the left in general and of communism in particular. Speaking at the EETPU's 1983 conference he said "it is my personal dream that the two unions would soon merge." With undisguised glee the tabloids reported this aspiration. "Shock for the left" gloated the Mail On Sunday. "Two right wingers plan Britain's biggest union." The moderate controlled organisation was about to become a major influence on TUC and Labour Party policy making. An indication of the touching innocence of some sections of the British press when it comes to trade union matters. Terry Duffy and Frank Chapple may have been conducting a secret courtship but their organisations were a long way off making their relationship respectable.

For starters, the EETPU wanted a total merger of the two unions. It wanted to replace the Engineering Section's powerful district and divisional committees with its own industrial committees. It wanted all national officers to be elected by postal ballot conducted by the Electoral Reform Society. (The Engineering Section liked to run its own elections.) It wanted area officials to be elected or appointed in line with each union's practice and it wanted existing EETPU officials who had been appointed to have their contracts honoured. Finally, having rejected the Worthing proposals for a 300 and then a 150 strong national conference the Engineering Section was to be asked to agree to an enlargement of the 600 strong EETPU Biennial Conference.

In stark contrast to the reception it gave to the conditions that TASS had sought the Engineering Section leaders went out of their way to try and convince the members and the National Committee that the EETPU's terms could easily be accommodated. It seemed strange that they of all people should have disregarded the strong hold that craft fundamentalism had on the members of its leading committees. The National Committee rejected the EETPU out of hand. The much heralded "moderate-controlled organisation" did not after all materialise.

Eventually, agreement was reached on a new set of AUEW Rules to govern what had now become a two-section federation. The problem of mandating was dealt with. The TASS delegation to the National Conference was increased by taking into consideration the reality of its merger with the Sheet Metal Workers. The fear TASS expressed regarding the use of the 1964 Trade Union Act was eliminated by the availability of a mutual veto. But most significantly a new rule was added that provided for the dissolution of the two-section union - but not the sections - by a simple majority of either of the two-section policy bodies. The AUEW had acquired a fire escape.

Not too long after these rules were endorsed and approved by all concerned the inevitable occurred. At its 1985 National Committee Meeting the manual workers section of the AUEW carried by 75 votes to 48 a motion to dissolve the Federation. Normal trade union fraternal relations and formal functions and procedures were slowly but surely being eroded.

In TASS's book a union for engineering employees with a prominent and clearly identifiable white collar section would languish in an industrial cul-de-sac. In terms of the engineering industry TASS was in no doubt of the way ahead. But its left wing stance in defence of free collective bargaining and union independence resulted in an upsurge of reaction that discounted industrial logic the supporters of the motion referred to TASS as a cancer that had to be cut out. Terry Duffy claimed TASS never wanted amalgamation. "If you are seeking to apportion blame" he said "you should apportion all of it to TASS." Those who were opposed to the dissolution pleaded for the door to be kept open on the dream of one union for engineering workers. Mr Harry Cutts implored the delegates not to commit trade union suicide while Mr Ken Buxton warned that we needed TASS more than they needed us. When he received the news that his union was no longer under the AUEW umbrella, Ken Gill spoke of his sorrow that the wiser councils had not prevailed. "Their members will suffer from this breach, TASS is more than capable of looking after itself" he added.

TASS's apparent reconciliation to the situation was more a diplomatic response to something they had been waiting for for some time. Ken Gill knew very well that as soon as the Engineering Section found an acceptable means for getting rid of TASS it would use it. What the Engineering Section did not twig was that he was stringing out the discussions on his own suggestion of a two-section union and the consequent rule changes until the result of the Sheet Metal Workers ballot was known. Once that decision was taken TASS was independently viable.

Effectively, the 1976 National Committee of the Engineering Section with its combination of right wing ideologues and conservative "tool makers" put paid to any hopes of the AUEW ever becoming one union for all engineering workers. To form a union that was going to represent craft apprentices, office trainees, all those with varying levels of manual and non-manual skills, technicans, technologists, administrators and supervisors right up to middle management would have required completely new concepts of structure and conventions. The traditionalists would not entertain such dramatic changes, the political right dreaded their consequences.

Despite their cautiousness the draughtsmen were naturally open to new ideas. They were more acutely conscious of the effect of technological innovations than their blue collar colleagues, whose

TASS was compelled to promote its interests in other directions

structural changes in the sixties

Membership control was, at least in the opinion of active members, the quintessence of trade union democracy. Those who were on the Executive Committee were acutely conscious of the fact that their lay member status gave weight to the authority they exercised and the responsibility they carried. There were Freudian undertones in their relationship with the full-time officers. But as long as both groups understood who it was determined the union's policies and decided its priorities then everything was fine. Full-time officials, however, had much closer contact with a wider range of ordinary rank and file members. They were more likely to be identified as "the union" than the EC member. The rank and file were generally reassured when it was known that their grievances were being dealt with by a "professional". The full-time official had substantial influence.

DATA, and the AESD before it, relied on its system for the selection of full-time officers, producing individuals who would put service to the union before personal standing. The procedure was for a committee of lay members representing all the districts to be elected by the delegates at the Annual Conference. This committee would interview the candidates for a full-time post and make its choice. What they were looking for was someone with a track record as an active lay member and who showed an awareness of the economic, political and social conditions in which the Association operated. The delegates at the Annual Conference would then be given the opportunity to endorse or repudiate the selection. For AESD/DATA the difficulties caused by rapid growth began to manifest themselves halfway through the fifties. The full-time national and divisional officials were increasingly finding their physical resources being stretched to the limits.

All issues affecting the union at national level were at the time handled by three officials, the General Secretary G H Doughty, the Assistant General Secretary R Dickinson and the Editor J E Mortimer, who were located at Head Office in Richmond, Surrey. Out in the field were nine divisional organisers each responsible for two districts. Within the divisional boundaries an appropriate number of branches were co-ordinated by a lay member divisional council. Some districts had as many as 22 branches, Scotland for instance. The average number of branches per division was about ten.

Divisions 1 and 2 were covered by F H Stephen from an office in Glasgow. He had to be available to all the members in Scotland and Northern Ireland. Responsibility for Divisions 3 and 4 was carried by A M Baxter based in Leeds but more likely to be found working in either the North or North-East of England. J Forrester, operating from

Manchester, took in the North-West and the Lake District. The East Midlands down to the Wash was looked after by G Cornes, from an office in Nottingham. K M Kelly covered the heavily industrialised West Midlands and North Wales from and office in Birmingham. South Wales and the whole of the West Country were serviced from Bristol by G R Sale. London, the Home Counties and East Anglia were shared between W E Winterbottom, E D Southwell and R J Silverthorne.

By definition divisional organisers were expected to spend the most time recruiting and organising new members. In practice they were more likely to be found arguing across the table with managers or personnel officers trying to negotiate a settlement to a claim or a grievance. The procedural arrangements in the majority of companies where DATA was recognised required the full-time official to meet the management representatives if the domestic talks had failed to reach an agreement. The understanding between the union and the employers was that all procedural stages would have to be completed before either side took more drastic action. It was, therefore, essential for the divisional organisers to keep Head Office briefed on the state of every issue with which they were dealing. So besides writing up reports, attending branch meetings, two divisional councils, meetings of trades councils, inter-union conferences, weekend schools and preparing cases for industrial courts and tribunals, the divisional organisers had to spend long boring hours getting from one place to another. When there was a strike (and DATA's policies ensured that these would be frequent) the divisional organisers would have to spend a greater portion of their time keeping in touch with the strike committees and making sure they would be available if there should be signs of a settlement meeting. Sometimes experienced lay members would be called upon to deputise for the full-time official who might be pinned down somewhere else. It was through situations like this that many future candidates for a full-time post got the opportunity of building a reputation for themselves. But there was also the moot point of lay members getting time off from work and the question of compensation for loss of earnings that was usually a condition of their release. Coming into the sixties the stresses and strains of providing a comprehensive service to a continually increasing number of members were beginning to show.

In November 1961 things came to a head with the sudden death of the London Organiser, R J Silverthorne. Although he was considered by many to be an awkward customer, his contrariness sprang from the uncompromising principles of his socialist belief. His fierce criticisms were always aimed at ideas, never at individuals. And like so many of his kind he suffered when the ripostes were directed at a personal level.

This was the first time the Association was faced with one of its officials dying in office. Normally when an official was retiring or gave notice of resignation the procedure for getting a replacement would be put on the Agenda of the next Annual Conference. Then a selection committee would be elected and told to get on with the job of finding a new official. Once this committee had completed this exercise it stood down. Reg Silverthorne's death meant that a busy London Division would be without an organiser until well into the following year. Available lay members were pressed into service. The office staff struggled to do what they could. Members were beginning to complain about lack of service.

Within its structure the Association had an

Emergency Committee of the Representative Council, which was itself elected at the Annual RC Conference. It met infrequently and only when it was deemed necessary by the Executive Committee. The growing problems in Divisions 17 and 18 prompted the EC to exercise this option. On Saturday 25 November 1961 the Association's President, H Smith, and the Vice President, A W Day, accompanied by the General Secretary, G H Doughty, three members of the Executive Committee and eight regional representatives assembled at the Windsor Hotel, Lancaster Gate, London.

The "Digest of Proceedings" of this meeting conveyed the precision and meticulous attention to detail that draughtsmen bring to bear on what they perceive as a complex assignment. First of all they cleared the decks by formally constituting themselves under rule. They were indeed an Emergency Committee. The General Secretary was then called upon to make a report as to the circumstances which persuaded the EC to have the Committee convened. While claiming that he did not intend to make as long a statement as the one he had made to the EC about the "major organisational problems" facing the Association, Mr Doughty left no detail undefined in his "resume" of the predicament they appeared to be in. The committee members were presented with copies of a diagram, which was not surprising for an organisation of people whose trade was the production of graphic representations. The diagram showed (in the shaded portions) the periods when Mr Silverthorne had been absent from the Chiswick Office. There was the period of the court case (Rookes v Bernard), there was the period of his normal holidays (to which he was entitled), there was a period of illness during the course of which his wife died and for which he was granted an additional period of leave and after which he suffered a further period of illness. Finally, the period of absence during which Mr Silverthorne himself died immediately after he left hospital. Another diagram showed the details of the arrangements which were made to handle the work in the Division through the use of other officials and involving lay members. "Those temporary arrangements" said the General Secretary, "could not last too long". But be that as it may, the question the EC was asking was, was there an emergency?

The question was teased, tested and tried until each member of the committee cautiously agreed, not quite unanimously, but at least "nem con" that there was an emergency. Anyone who may have thought that having come a hard road to that conclusion it would be downhill from then on would have revealed their lack of appreciation of the nature of the technical mind. Agreeing that something would have to be done about it was one thing, but what? And how? These were two other things altogether.

With a reverence for nuance and a feeling for semantics which would have won the approval of a school of medieval theologians, the committee laboriously reached a decision. There would be a special gathering of the Representative Council on the same conditions as its normal Annual Conference. There arrangements would be made to appoint a fulltime official to fill the vacancy in the Chiswick Office "on the same salary and conditions as apply to other Divisional Organisers".

Content that the committee had driven home every dot over each "i" and that every "t" had been transfixed with a reinforced bar, the President declared the meeting closed: as the digest put it "The proceedings then terminated." The ultra-careful observation of the rule book was not just a characteristic of draughtsmen. The administration of craft-based unions tends to reflect this preoccupation with fine detail which their members apply in their occupations.

The special Representative Council Meeting was held on 6 January 1962 at the Beaver Hall, London EC4. The single item on the Agenda was the election of a committee to select a new full-time official. From the 175 delegates came 29 nominations to fill nine places. Scheduled to finish at 5.30pm the election procedure went on until after 6pm with the President appealing to delegates to remain as long as possible to ensure a quorum when the results were announced. The committee which was finally elected was made up of six EC members, two members of the Standing Orders Committee and a branch delegate. In political terms it was split 50-50 between individuals who were seen to be either right or left wingers. Later in January they interviewed the candidates and selected Mr R Woolf. Dick Woolf's record of fourteen years service on the Executive Committee along with the fact that he had done the lion's share of the work when the Chiswick Office was under resourced was sufficient to overcome any prejudice which may have arisen from the fact that he was a member of the Communist Party.

No sooner was the vacancy arising from the death of one official filled when the news came through that Mr G R Sale, the Divisional Organiser for the West Country had died. George Sale was only 48 when a severe illness ended his life. He was respected for his loyalty to the Association and for the tenacity with which he dealt with members' problems. Politically he was probably to the right of the current trends developing in the union. Nevertheless, he always acknowledged that it was his job to ensure that policies determined through the democracy of the Association were carried out.

With the Annual Conference due to take place in April it was not necessary for the Emergency Committee to meet. This time the delegates were asked by the Executive Committee not only to replace Mr Sale but also to give the go- ahead for the appointment of two new divisional organisers for centres to be opened in Liverpool and Newcastle-upon-Tyne. Mr F J Ticehurst of Southampton, a member of the Executive Committee, was appointed in June 1962 to fill the vacancy in the Bristol Office.

The EC had indicated its preferences for the redistribution of branches. On behalf of the EC the General Secretary pointed out that the proposals on the table were by way of an interim report. It was essential, in the opinion of the EC, that the two new offices should be opened immediately as these were the locations where need was greatest. The Newcastle office would take some of the strain off the Glasgow official, Mr F Stephen and the Liverpool office would also relieve him in Northern Ireland. "In its final report the EC might have other proposals to put before Conference in connection with the question of Divisional Offices and Divisional Organisation."

The first amendment came from the Glasgow South delegate, Mr A McAlpine, and was supported by the Mayfair delegate, R Huzzard. They wanted four not two new organisers appointed. The former argued that more officials were needed to concentrate on recruitment and organisation rather then act as "paid negotiators." The latter drew attention to the vast area of the country south of a line from the Wash to the tip of Pembroke which had to be covered by only two officials. The supporting speeches recounted the desperate plight of divisional organisers risking life and limb to make meetings which were hundreds of miles apart. The General Secretary in reply stated that the EC was fully aware of the problems but wanted time to examine the various situations more thoroughly. The amendment was defeated. The second amendment, like in a Dutch auction, proposed three new officials. The same arguments were restated by different people only defining the problems in different parts of the country. They received the same reply from the General Secretary with the same outcome.

There followed nine further amendments to the Executive's proposals regarding the reshuffling of the branches. Six were lost, each one only getting the support of the region it affected. The three which were carried showed that the Executive Committee was not totally indifferent to special pleading; when it was of marginal significance.

The September issue of the "Draughtsman" announced that two new divisional organisers had been appointed by the Selection Committee. They were Mr Brian Richardson of Nottingham Branch and Mr Ken Gill of Edgware. Both were members of the EC and according to the report were in their middle thirties but despite their youth had very considerable experience at office, branch, district and national level of the Association. The reassurance in this statement was appropriate in an organisation which only admitted people to full membership when they had attained the age of 25.

In January 1963 Ken Gill was posted in the new divisional office in Liverpool with responsibility for North West England and the North of Ireland. By February Brian Richardson was in charge of the Leeds office while its previous encumbent, Alex Baxter took over in Newcastle-upon-Tyne.

Instead of having just nine organisers, each with two divisions to look after, there were now eleven. And those in Glasgow, Newcastle, Leeds and Manchester had one division only.

At the 1963 Annual Conference the Association took its first, albeit carefully considered, step to free itself of the constrictions which the AESD had been imposing on the development of the organisational structure. A rule change allowed each conference to elect a selection committee for the appointment of full-time officials when and where they were needed. There would no longer be either the requirement to await for another conference to be held or the need for the tedious arguments which took place on the emergency committee. In 1965 the rule concerning the emergency committee was changed and the committee ceased to exist.

The Association expanded its divisional organisation in 1964 by opening offices in Gloucester and Chelmsford. Mr Harry Smith from Yorkshire, who had been President of the Association when it changed its title to DATA in 1961, was appointed to the Gloucester office and another member of the Executive Committee, Mr John Tuchfeld to Chelmsford.

The establishment of fourteen divisions meant a slight reduction in the size of the EC. Now Ken Gill was the only organiser who had two divisions to look after. A number of rule changes agreed at the 1963 Annual Conference loosened up some of the bureaucracy which affected the work of the divisional councils and branches. Needless to say, every proposed change to traditional practice got the microscopic examination which draughtsmen were so expert at carrying out. Every nit was well and truly picked.

Typical, was the contretemps which occurred when a recommendation, approved at the 1962 Conference, came up for the appropriate rule change in 1963. Tradition had it that the annual conference of the representative council was held on the four days of the Easter holiday. With the growth in membership and the expansion of the Association the proposal was that the conference should be held on the first week in May. The Chair of the Standing

STEPPING OUT... Divisional Organiser Ken Gill joins DATA strikers from AEI Larne on a march through Belfast.

Orders Committee announced that this created a difficulty but it was not an emergency and, therefore, could not be corrected by means of an emergency motion. There were three ways of dealing with the situation according to the Standing Orders Committee. Accept what the report said and hold the next conference in the first week in May. Or reject the report and revert to the normal Easter date. Or refer back to the EC that part of the report which indicated the period when Conference would be held and let the EC submit a rule revision to the 1964 Conference with the present arrangement continuing for one year only. Nothing could be more up the draughtsmen's street than this feast of constitutional niceties. If Walter Bagehot had lived to hear the dissertations he would have ended up drumming his lips with his fingertips. It is sufficient to say that the Conference in 1964 was held in the first week in May and lasted five days.

During 1965 a sub-committee was set up to look after the future development of the Association. The fall in membership which had occurred in 1963 had been halted and reversed. With 64,000 members and still growing the pressure was on for additional officials and a still more flexible bureaucracy. When the annual conference met in Bournemouth in 1966 the sub-committee had its report ready for the approval of the delegates.

Its proposals were mostly concerned with image building and the pursuance of possible mergers with other unions in order to create a single white collar technical union in private and public industries. This was the period when discussions with the Scientific Workers and the Technical Civil Servants appeared to be progressing along favourable lines.

The concrete recommendations in the report were to divide Scotland into two divisions and appoint an extra official in Glasgow and to open new offices in Coventry and Belfast, providing two officials to relieve Birmingham and Liverpool of some of their workload. It would have been naive of the EC to think that these proposals would get through without amendment. Yet, although there were some long-winded statements over details, the amendments which were carried merely amounted to fine tuning and the report was accepted almost as written.

In March 1967 A McAlpine, who was President of DATA in 1964/65, took over the new office in Glasgow. B Graham and G Hope, both of whom had been senior divisional council members, were appointed to Belfast and Coventry respectively. The Association had expanded to sixteen regional divisions each with a single organiser.

Later that year on 28 October Eric Southwell, the organiser for the South London region died. He was 47 years of age, had served in the Royal Artillery in the Second World War and returned to the engineering industry on being demobbed. His contribution to the Association as an active lay member was acknowledged when he became a divisional organiser in 1957. Because of his fluency in French, German and Italian, Eric had represented the Association at a number of European industrial conferences. Once again the Selection Committee went into action and chose G W Strattan to fill the vacancy. The Executive Committee then acceded to a request from K Gill, the Liverpool organiser, to transfer to London. George Strattan took over the Liverpool position.

In 1965 an interesting and somewhat surprising development in the Association's organisation took place. From the early twenties the draughtsmen and tracers in the Republic of Ireland were organised in the Association of Engineering and Shipbuilding

Draughtsmen. The fact that the Association eventually affiliated to the British Labour Party did not bother these Irish members too much at the time. However, the problems came when in 1949 the Labour Government passed an amendment to the 1920 Ireland Bill in which it undertook to uphold the constitutional position of the Six County area of Northern Ireland. Members from the Irish Republic believed that the AESD ought to have disassociated itself from what they saw was confirmation of imperialist occupation of their country. At a general meeting held in Dublin to discuss the issue, the General Secretary of the AESD, James Young, stated that the union would stand by the decision of the Labour Government. The upshot was that a ballot of the members was taken on whether or not they should remain in the Association under these circumstances. The majority was for severing connection with the AESD.

Efforts were made to build a wholly Irish-based union for engineering technical staff. The new organisation Cumann Teichneoiri Innealtoireachta, the CTI (loosely translated as The Union of Engineering Technicians), was structured along the same lines as the AESD. It affiliated to the Irish Transport and General Workers' Union as an autonomous body responsible for its own industrial group. In spite of an enthusiastic start, the demands on the lay officials (it could not afford full-timers) the difficulties of building an engineering white-collar union in a mainly agricultural economy and certain difficulties arising from its ITGWU arrangements eventually led to its demise.

Whatever their political differences with the British union, the leading members of the CTI kept in touch with the national officers of the AESD. When that organisation became the Draughtsmen's and Allied Technicians' Association, George Doughty, the DATA General Secretary was approached to see if there would be any chance of bringing the Draughtsmen's Union back to the Republic. The differences of opinion on the Irish question were no longer the stumbling block they had been in the past. There was no argument on the DATA EC over the desirability of re-establishing the Association in the whole of Ireland. Nevertheless, a view was expressed, principally by the Editor, J E Mortimer, that the ultimate aim of DATA should be to help the Irish Technical Staffs to build their own independent organisation. As this was seen as a very long term objective it did not in any way delay the Executive Committee from responding positively to the Irish approach.

A publicly-advertised meeting was held in the Gresham Hotel, O'Connell Street, Dublin. There was a distinguished platform from DATA including the President - T Young, Vice President - R Whitley, General Secretary - G Doughty, General Treasurer - N Hare along with K Gill, who was then the Divisional Organiser for Liverpool and Northern Ireland, Brian Graham - the Northern Ireland Divisional Council Secretary and a number of leading members of the Northern Ireland Divisional Council.

A resolution was formally moved and unanimously agreed that a Dublin branch of DATA would be established. The branch officials were elected. 120 application forms were completed there and then.

The bulk of this new membership were draughtsmen employed in the Irish Electricity Supply Board. In November of 1965 the Board put forward its plan for staff reorganisation. The technical staff saw in the proposals a serious deterioration in their pay and conditions compared to other staff categories. The subsequent dispute between the new DATA union and the Electricity Supply Board reached the headlines when it seemed there were threats of a nationwide electricity blackout. An eleventh-hour intervention by the Irish Congress of Trade Unions brought a settlement. The draughtsmen and technicians in the ESB preserved their position in the wage league and everybody was talking about this new union.

Flushed with the success of the union's ESB members, twelve draughtsmen and one tracer in Ireland's machine won peat industry, Bord na Mona, came out on strike in October 1966. Little did they think that in spite of enormous support from the union and its Irish membership seven months would pass before a settlement and a return to work would be achieved. Bitter disputes were a feature of the union's early days in the Republic, an indication of the industrial relations problems created by the years when there was no effective staff organisation. As it did in the UK DATA was demonstrating its willingness to back members in fighting grievances with their employers. The culture, the accents and the environment were different but the conflict of interests was the same. The Association was making its mark on the Irish trade union scene.

In 1969 George Doughty was able to announce to the Union's RC Annual Conference at Bournemouth that by a majority of two to one over 500 graduate engineers, also from the Electricity Supply Board, Dublin, had voted to join DATA and formed Dublin's No.2 branch. Other groups of engineers became interested and another engineers branch was established in Limerick.

The Irish membership continued to grow both in numbers and confidence. Those who were encouraged by the emphasis which DATA placed on lay member control began to make a significant contribution to the Association's policy-making processes and on its administrative committees. There was no doubt that the re-introduction of DATA into the Republic of Ireland was a success. The long term question of an independent Irish Technical Staff Union remains on the table.

1970 saw the Association membership climb above the 100,000 mark. External criticism of its "communist-dominated leadership and its militant left-wing policies" were not deterring engineering technical staff from joining its ranks. Efficient and effective service to the members was a more significant element of its image than its political posture. "A most spectacular year" enthused the Annual Report of the Executive Committee to the 1970 Annual Conference. "This union has added 11,035 to the number of members on its books compared with 1968". It went on "It is a record year compared with any previous year."

But when George Doughty rose to present the EC's report on reorganisation he found he had to take brickbats rather than bows. He explained that successful recruitment over a wider field of technical staff and a high level of industrial activity were the main reasons compelling the EC to carry out a major examination of the Association's structure. This would be completed in time for the 1971 Conference. In the interim the EC was proposing that two more divisional organisers would be appointed.

"Not good enough" rejoined D Daunt from Liverpool South Branch. "1971 was too far away". A countrywide reorganisation was needed now. The delegate from East Devon, K Appleby, moved reference back of the whole of the report. In other words, take it back and do it again. Speakers trooped to the rostrum complaining about the stresses and strains active members were having to bear in filling the gaps in the structure and retailing incidences where recruitment opportunities were being lost through the shortage of full-time officials. The ultra-left purists, who were, unusually, supporting the EC, called instead for greater involvement of lay members and less full-time official "domination."

George Doughty met the challenge head on. "Where would a reference back get them?" he asked. "Did they want to give the EC authority in the matter of full-time officials which they never had before?" "Did they not want the branches to have a chance of discussing the new proposals before they came to conference next year?"

The EC was asking Conference to add two more officials immediately and to accept that after everybody had the opportunity of discussing and consulting with each other about what should be done, there would be a full programme of divisional reorganisation and an increase in the number of officials the following year.

The delegates could not question this involvement of the broad democratic processes and rejected the reference back. They then went ahead and agreed to the setting up of two new divisions, one based in the Dorset, Hampshire and Sussex area and the other in West Midlands. The offices were opened in Southampton and Rugeley in Stafford. The former to be run by K Lane, an activist who worked in Rolls-Royce Bristol Engines and the latter by W B Shields, a past president of the union and an active member in Ayrshire. DATA now had eighteen divisions.

At its Richmond headquarters there were still just three national officials. The only change was in the person of the Editor. When J E Mortimer resigned to take up a position on the Prices and Incomes Board the Annual Conference delegates were recalled on 12 October 1968 to decide on the appointment of a successor. Applications were invited and in December K Gill was chosen by the Selection Committee. The resulting vacancy in the South London Division was filled in April 1969 by L Formby, the EC Member for the Liverpool Region.

During the time the planning and reorganisation proposals were being thought out a situation occurred in the Glasgow South Divisional Office which ended with the Selection Committee having to be re-convened. F H Stephen, after fifteen years service as Divisional Organiser in Scotland submitted his resignation to the Executive Committee. An inquiry into reasons for him taking this drastic step was put in the hands of the President - G Clay, the Vice President - M Cooley, the Past President - K Banks and the General Secretary - G H Doughty. What they unravelled was an imbroglio of Byzantine proportions from which it emerged that the relationship between Mr Stephen and prominent lay members of the Divisional Council had reached a position which was beyond repair.

The EC came to the conclusion that "no further efforts be made to reconcile the irreconcilable." And although Mr Stephen indicated he was prepared to withdraw his resignation the EC stated that to agree to that would not be in the best interests of the union or Mr Stephen. The final report on the matter included what amounted to a code of practice covering the relationship between lay activists and full-time officials.

At the 1971 Annual Conference at which the EC's decisions were endorsed G Cornes, speaking on behalf of the divisional organisers, paid tribute to Mr Stephen's work for the union in twenty-five years as a lay and full-time official.

With the appointment of W Niven, the Scottish EC Member to the Glasgow South Office, the Association was poised for one of the most far reaching re-organisations exercised in its history.

the 1971 reorganisation

The 1970 Annual Conference had expressed the urgent need for something to be done to enable the Association to cope with the greatly increased membership (over 100,000 and still growing). After studying the wide range of ideas, suggestions and comments from the localities and regions, from individual members and full-time officials, the EC circulated its report. This was then formally presented to the conference at Eastbourne in 1971. The main proposals related to divisional organisation with a consequent reordering of branches and to the organisation at the Head Office in Richmond. Needless to say the fine-combing the report got in the branches produced a crop of amendments. There were nineteen in all including one from the Executive itself which merely added that the changes should be completed within six months of them being adopted.

In his outline of the thinking behind the EC's re-organisation plan George Doughty, the General Secretary, pointed to the effects on the membership of changing technology and of the amalgamation with the three manual unions. It was evident that the Association was straining to service its members with inadequate resources. It badly needed more regional centres, more officials and more staff. Providing these would be costly but the expense could be met by having the means of realising the recruitment potential. The basic proposal was to bring the number of divisions up from 18 to 26 and redistribute the branches to achieve a rational balance in numbers and locations. With regard to the situation at Head Office, the General Secretary drew attention to the fact that in order to cope with the work load some officials were working from seven in the morning to eleven at night and foregoing holidays and weekends. The creation of a new post of Deputy General Secretary, splitting the administrative secretaries with supporting staffs and increasing research facilities, was essential. The further changes proposed were the restructuring of the Political and Industrial sub-committees of the Executive and finally a new name for the Association.

The amendments to the EC proposals were about the location of branches in the reconstituted divisions. Six were approved, nine were defeated, one was remitted and two were withdrawn. When it came to the EC's own amendment that the reorganisation should be completed in six months the General Secretary asked the delegates to allow it to be withdrawn. The time scale, he said, only referred to the divisional organisation and not to the head office arrangements which were critical. The EC would instead give an undertaking to implement the changes as soon as possible. The delegates would have none of it. Some of them said the EC was stalling to save money, an accusation that was hotly denied. Said one delegate, there was no excuse for withdrawing the amendment. If the target of six months could not be met the EC would have to explain why. The amendment stood.

The proposals regarding the appointment of a Deputy General Secretary and the consequent redefining of the duties of Head Office officials along with appropriate rule changes received the two-thirds majority approval. A short discussion did take place on an amendment suggesting that the General Secretary should be elected in the same way as the lay divisional council secretaries. It got no support. But it might have been an unconscious premonition that caused W Boyle, the delegate from Glasgow South, to raise the question of the difference between the Association's method of selecting officials and that of the manual unions with which it had decided to amalgamate.

In July the Selection Committee appointed Ken Gill to the newly elected post of Deputy General Secretary. His successor as Editor of the Journal was Harry Smith who had been the Divisional Organiser operating from the Gloucester office. At its October meeting as well as noting the serious effects of unemployment and the drain on union finances the Executive Committee placed eight new officers in new divisional offices. Of these, only Bill Sales had been an EC member. He took over in Leeds from Brian Richardson who had requested a transfer to the new Sheffield Office. The other officials were Don Carr who followed Harry Smith in the Gloucester office, Tony Foley went to Ipswich, John Jones to Pontypridd, Ron Longworth to Teeside, Jim McConnachie to Leicester, Norman McIntosh to Edinburgh, Jack Rice to Preston and John Rowan to North London. The Association now had the same number of divisions as the Amalgamated Engineering Union but with slightly different boundaries. It had thirty full-time officials.

There was no opposition to the name change. The title was to be the Technical and Supervisory Section of the Amalgamated Union of Engineering Workers. However, at its November meeting the EC took a decision to encourage the use of the initials TASS, meaning the Technical, Administrative and Supervisory Section. At the 1973 Annual Conference that title was made official.

Draughtsmen who represented the heart and mind of the union were being forced to accelerate the programme of re-organisation which would reflect their own diminishing role in the engineering industry. The structures and services that they had initially devised were adequate for members whose working conditions placed them in numbers within a single office space. Identifying themselves as a collective was easy. There were no communication difficulties. But it was a set-up that now appealed only to members who chose to disregard the pace at which the technology was eradicating time-honoured methods of production. For the activists there were two factors that would not go away. One was the division of labour creating new job functions in planning, design and research and the other was the intensity of the competition between unions recruiting in the expanding white collar sectors. It was clear to all but the more esoteric organisations that only big battalions of labour had any chance in achieving their objectives in an economy dominated by massive combines and transnational corporations.

The measures taken by the AESD and DATA in the face of industrial developments were to say the least, circumspect. TASS had ground to make up. It would have to act decisively if it was going to remain an effective union. It could be said that the

1971 Conference agreeing to bring the number of officials in the field up to twenty-six was a sign things were on the move. The appointment of one more national official at Head Office, in the person of a Deputy General Secretary, was more prudent.

Two years later at Bournemouth, George Doughty, General Secretary since 1952, announced that he would be retiring after the 1974 Annual Conference. The delegates approved an EC recommendation that the Selection Committee, which was about to appoint successors to three divisional organisers due to retire, should also appoint a General Secretary and fill any consequential vacancies.

In July the Committee announced its decisions. Ken Gill became General Secretary Elect to take up the position when George Doughty retired. The appointment of the three new organisers resulted in a series of changes. Firstly, Arthur Scott, who had been the General Treasurer, replaced Alec Baxter in Newcastle-upon-Tyne. Les Thomas, an experienced activist from Merseyside, was prevented by illness from moving as planned to the Rugeley Office (in place of William Shields who was to be transferred to the Birmingham Office on the retirement of Ken Kelly). Vernon Gapper, the EC member for South Wales succeeded George Cornes in Nottingham. The Committee also selected the Manchester Divisional Organiser, John Forrester to take up the post of Deputy General Secretary after Ken Gill. Jim Fairly, who was active in the Gateshead area was appointed to fill the consequent vacancy in the Manchester Office. He started, however, by holding the fort at Rugeley.

In response to the increased workload and demands from the membership the 1974 Annual Conference approved the appointment of two more divisional organisers without increasing the number of divisions. One was to be located in the Birmingham office with responsibility for the serving of members employed by BLMC, Lucas, GEC and Dunlop, the other would open a proposed new office in Dublin serving members in the Republic of Ireland and reporting to the No.4 Divisional Council.

Due to the continued serious illness of Les Thomas one of the newly appointed officials, Jack Carr, the EC member for the North East Division, was placed temporarily in the Rugeley office. The intention was that he would take over the North London office when its current official, John Rowan became the Combines Organiser in the West Midlands. Regrettably, Les Thomas's illness persisted and in the end he had to inform the EC that he would be unable to carry out the responsibilities of the job. This meant Jack Carr remained in Rugeley.

Brian Anderson, the Irish EC Member was appointed as Divisional Organiser for the office in Dublin.

DATA and wage restraint

When the going gets tough in a capitalist economy the convention is to air the problems in generalities - "we are not producing enough", "we are importing more than we are exporting", "we are spending more than we are earning", "we are pricing ourselves out of the market", and so on and so on. When the going gets tougher and things seem to be getting out of control, then the plain generalities become specific generalities, - "the unions are to blame", "unions are behaving irresponsibly", "something has to be done about the unions". Not any particular union, just the unions. The received wisdom is that all the complexities and inter-relationships of a country's financial, industrial and social structures can be distilled to a single, simple notion that the economic problems which arise in capitalism can be laid at the door of the organised working class.

The 1961 version of a capitalist crisis was about an adverse trade balance. The British people were, it seemed, buying more and more imported goods and selling less and less of their own manufactures abroad. The remedy, according to the government of Harold MacMillan, was to raise the bank rate to 7 per cent, restrict credit facilities and introduce a wage freeze, euphemistically referred to as "a pay pause."

To show where it stood with regard to the government's policies, the union's journal carried editorials which contrasted the demands on wage incomes compared with dividend incomes and fed the members with all the statistical evidence they needed to press on with claims for increases in pay, pause or no pause. DATA was 100 per cent behind the General Secretary of the Transport Workers Union, Frank Cousins, who stated at the 1961 Labour Party Annual Conference "We are not willing to accept in any form, shape or disguise, wage restraint."

The pay pause, such as it was, lasted until March 1962. The government then tried to compel a 2.5 per cent limit on wage increases. DATA continued to encourage members to go for as much as they could. To sustain its militant policy on wages the EC made an urgent appeal to the membership to accept a higher subscription rate, plus a levy. DATA was demonstrating its total rejection of incomes policies. Likewise, at its 1962 Annual Conference DATA rejected out of hand the decision of the TUC to go along with the newly- formed National Economic Development Council. In the opinion of the Association NEDDY was one of Frank Cousin's disguised forms of wage restraint.

The measures taken by the government did nothing to alleviate the strains on the economy. Things went from bad to worse. Unemployment was on the increase, particularly in the North of the country. The freezing winter of 1962/63 did nothing to help the situation. The building trades suffered very badly. DATA was not to escape from the effects of these economic factors. The steep rise in the unemployment benefit being paid out showed what was happening. In 1960 the unemployment benefit payment for the year cost the Association £6,715. In 1962 this had climbed to £40,853. As was expected, unemployment became one of the big topics at the 1963 Annual Conference.

A motion from Crawley Branch, supported by Coventry East and Bristol, called for the opening of national level negotiations with the employers for an agreement on redundancy procedure. This would involve maximum consultations before any redundancy took place and minimum redundancy payments based on length of service. The motion was defeated. Those who spoke against it insisted it was the job of the union to press for full employment not to provide a policy for unemployment. "Besides", it was stated, "minimum terms usually become the maximum available.

From Salford Branch came a lengthy motion which laid down a militant strategy for tackling the problem. Unemployment, said the mover, could only be eliminated by the overthrow of the capitalist system. The trade union movement should be mobilised to fight redundancy wherever it appeared. The motion read like a socialist manifesto - the aims of which the EC fully supported. But in practical terms it did not allow the degree of flexibility needed in a union where the members showed a wide difference in their levels of political consciousness. The motion was remitted. The Conference did approve a resolution which allowed the EC to instruct all members that no overtime should be worked in firms where members were redundant without first consulting with the divisional organiser.

Unemployment benefits peaked to £41,455 in 1963 but fell back to £7,359 in 1964. It was 1967 before they once again surged up to almost £1,000 per week.

In the autumn of 1964 the Tory Government decided to put its handling of the economy to the country. The electorate responded by returning a Labour Government under its new leader, Harold Wilson, with an overall majority of four. The Wilson election campaign had been built around its commitment to develop and expand technology and put the nation's industrial output ahead of its rivals, "the technological revolution." Losing no time the Labour Administration set up a Ministry of Technology under the T&GWU Leader Frank Cousins, a Department of Education and Science, and a Department of Economic Affairs. It was all systems go to carry out the great national plan. There was a strongly held view among labour politicians that any policy with the word 'planning' in it was a clear indication that we were into the socialist millenium.

The General Council of the TUC was made aware through press leaks that the government was planning some form of legislation to curb wage increases. At a meeting held just before the 1965 Annual Congress, the General Council decided to issue a supplementary report in which it advocated the setting up of a TUC wage-vetting system and thereby making any legislation unnecessary.

When the report was presented at Congress the Boilermakers Society and DATA moved a counter proposal. As far as they were concerned both TUC wage-vetting and legislation would interfere with traditional trade union collective bargaining procedures and in the end lead to even more problems for the Labour Government and the TUC. What the Boilermakers and DATA were looking for was more planned investment in the economy to create jobs, raise living standards and to redistribute the wealth of the country in favour of the working class. By almost four million votes Congress rejected this proposal and carried the General Council's Report with a majority of about two million.

At the 1965 Labour Party Conference, the Secretary of State for the Department of Economic Affairs, George Brown, called for "planning by consent" with agreement between Government, Unions and Employers. "Socialists reject the law of the jungle" he declared, "we must insist that some workers must hold back while others go forward." However it may be described, what was coming over the horizon was wage regulation. The government was asking the trade union movement to show the same enthusiasm as the CBI for pay increases to be related to productivity. The function of the newly established National Prices and Incomes Review Board would be to operate an "early warning" system to give notice that increases were on the way. This would be made possible through the unions giving the Board advance notification of claims for improvement in members' pay and conditions of employment.

Immediately following the Secretary of State's speech, the Conference dealt with an emergency motion moved by ASSET and seconded by DATA. Clive Jenkins and George Doughty, the respective General Secretaries of the two unions, warned the delegates of the consequences of this advanced warning scheme. It would, in their opinion, inevitably lead to the introduction of authoritative legislation to prevent unions from carrying out what George Doughty described as "their normal and socially necessary functions," getting wage increases for their members through collective bargaining. It stood to reason, in the opinion of the two general secretaries, that if the Board intended to be an effective instrument of control it would have to have power to sanction a union which might disregard its findings. "Will there be fines? Will there be imprisonments?" asked Clive Jenkins.

Conference was not prepared to accept this logic and after a reassuring statement by the Chancellor of the Exchequer, Mr James Callaghan, the emergency motion was defeated, in a card vote 3,635,000 against and 2,540,000 for.

A carefully argued pamphlet on incomes policy, entitled "Declaration of Dissent," was published jointly by DATA, the Association of Scientific Workers, the Association of Supervisory Staffs Executives and Technicians, the Association of Cinematograph and Television Technicians and the Society of Technical Civil Servants. It was mainly the work of DATA Journal Editor, J E Mortimer and ASSET General Secretary, Clive Jenkins. The pamphlet was widely circulated among the membership and in the broad trade union movement. It reassured all those who believed that trade unions in a capitalist society needed all the freedom they could get if they were to meet the aspirations of their members.

Harold Wilson saw little chance of implementing Labour's promised programme of social and economic reform with his fragile majority. He wanted a proper mandate. There was only one way to get it. Early in 1966 he announced there was to be another General Election - polling day 31 March.

The voters were persuaded to give him the opportunity he badly wanted. Labour was returned to power, this time with a comfortable parliamentary majority of 97.

Within a matter of months there was a wage freeze and a Prices and Incomes Act. Besides compelling unions to give early warning of proposed

CAPITAL GAIN... Strikers march in London to support wage claims, above. Right, **members picket outside Grantham vehicle makers Barfords, demanding the union-negotiated pay rates**

DEMONSTRATING SOLIDARITY... Picket, top, **outside the main gates of Hopkinsons Ltd in Huddersfield, November 1961 and,** above, **a support march in the same dispute.** Right, **Ken Gill addresses DATA members locked out of GEC, Preston, as they lobby the TUC Conference in Blackpool.**

wage claims. Part 4 of the Act gave employers the legal right to break negotiated contracts for the introduction of higher pay for the same work. It also made it unlawful for a worker or trade union to take any action or threaten action to force an employer to implement an award when it was forbidden by a Government Order. The Association's very raison d'etre as a wage fighting machine was being seriously hampered by the policies of a Labour Government. Editorials in DATA's journal expressed its indignation. Motions from the EC to the TUC deplored the provisions of the Act pointing out they were damaging to the interests of all trade unionists. DATA sponsored MPs Mr E Bishop and Mr A Booth were briefed to voice the union's opposition in the House.

Although there were no departmental orders giving employers a legal right to get out of payment of wage increases, many took the opportunity to either put into cold storage or cancel agreements which had been negotiated. "Monstrous" was how the DATA Journal described these actions. The Executive Committee rejected any suggestion of taking the issue to court and instead promised that it would officially support any group of members who took their claims through the recognised procedures as far as possible. DATA members at C A Parsons Ltd, Newcastle-upon-Tyne, the Triangle Valve Co Ltd, and Dewrance & Co Ltd, Warrington went on strike in September and October 1966 to get a four-week holiday entitlement.

Each of these strikes went grinding on into 1967 without interference from the government or, for that matter, from the employers. Holiday improvements were eventually secured. The ending of the wage freeze in December 1966 was followed by a period of "severe restraint." The criteria which justified a wage increase only applied to workers who were on the lowest pay levels or to those who could demonstrate they had contributed to an increase in productivity. DATA was not slow to point out that the pay offered to young draughtsmen and designers was too low to attract suitable workshop apprentices into the drawing office. As for the mature members, the union claimed the very nature of their job was to improve productivity only there were no means by which their contribution could be directly measured.

By August 1967 some form of voluntary restraint was supposed to be in operation, a system which had no attraction to DATA. In the meantime, the Engineering Employers' Federation had conscientiously observed the Labour Government's pay policy. That meant the National Minimum Rates for draughtsmen remained unchanged since 1965. When negotiations began in 1967 the employers' offer was so far from the figure which DATA delegates had determined at their Annual Conference and the strings attached so restrictive, a breakdown was inevitable. DATA declared that the National Agreement was terminated and members would be encouraged to go for substantial increases at domestic level.

Apparently members in a large number of firms were doing just that. "Apparently", because each month the Executive Committee was publishing the successful results of domestic negotiations from all over the country but without naming the companies involved. "A firm in Scotland" or "a firm in the North East" or "a firm in the South West" was the formula used to convey the terms of settlements. It was further claimed that many of these rises were in excess of the offer made by the Engineering Employers' representatives at the abortive national level discussions. The anonymity ploy was meant to prevent the Prices and Incomes Board finding out whether the increases met with its conditions. The DATA Journal's customary photographs of members on picket duty or marching in demonstrations showed little regard for such tactful reticence.

On 20 June 1968 agreement was reached at last with the Engineering Employers on a scale of minimum rates for draughtsmen and tracers. These ranged from £19.50 per week at age 21 to £25.50 per week at age 30 and over for draughtsmen. For the tracers, £11.00 per week at age 19 to £15.00 per week at 25 and over. It had a clause inserted to indicate that it was intended to offset the cost of the settlement by "the effective use of manpower" and "the introduction of new methods." It also stated that unless it heard otherwise from the First Secretary of the Department of Employment and Productivity the agreement would be implemented on 22 July. Barbara Castle's silence on this matter was not an indication of ministerial indifference to the affairs of a relatively narrow-based union. In that very same month her offer of a position on the Prices and Incomes Board to J E Mortimer, the Editor of DATA Journal was accepted.

Jim Mortimer had been an emphatic critic of incomes policies and an outstanding defender of free collective bargaining. Intellectually he stood head and shoulders above the vast majority of trade union apologists. Most DATA activists bathed frankly in the reflective glory of his contributions on major working class issues. His defection to an institution concerned with wage regulation was a severe blow and at the time, deeply resented. In time and on reflection the mood of the DATA leadership changed from anger to regret.

As a conscientious and deep thinking officer of the union Jim Mortimer had for a long time to endure a continuous barrage of the kind of non-specific criticism that emanated from the ultra left. Certain prominent EC members who were possibly envious of Jim's standing in the movement or perhaps incapable of comprehending his breadth of vision tried to ridicule or impute sinister motives to any suggestions or proposals he might make at Executive Committee meetings.

No one could have been more sensitive to the apparent contradiction of a committed opponent of incomes policy becoming part of the Prices and incomes Board than Jim Mortimer himself. In the end he reasoned that if the Board was going to be a fact of industrial life the vacancy on it would be better filled by a person with his understanding of the problems of trade unions.

When the TUC celebrated its centenary in September 1968 at Blackpool, Jenny Lee had the job of conveying fraternal greetings from the Labour Party to the delegates. There was a certain amount of reserve in their response. She may have obtained some comfort when a resolution, backed by DATA, which sharply criticised the Government's economic policies, was defeated. If that were the case it did not last very long. With the exception of Les Cannon of the ETU, the big trade union guns in the persons of Frank Cousins of the Transport Workers, Hugh Scanlon of the Engineering Workers, Danny MacGarvey of the Boilermakers and Clive Jenkins of the Managers and Technicians blasted the Labour Government's Prices and Incomes Policy. Hugh Scanlon, drawing on his knowledge of the Bible, quoted Matthew 25, Verse 29: "Unto everyone that hath shall be given and he shall have abundance: but from him that hath not, shall be taken away even that which he hath." "I have always felt" he said "that one of the best methods of gauging the success or otherwise of a trade union is by examining how effectively it alters the situation as described by St Matthew". George Doughty, newly elected to the

General Council, in more didactic tones pointed out that the Labour Government was imposing measures, enforced with unprecedented legal sanctions, on the 93 per cent of the population that had to share only 16 per cent of the national wealth. By over 7 million votes to a mere 1 million Congress rejected Government interference in collective bargaining. It then barely accepted the General Council's "voluntary vetting system." The majority in favour was around 30,000.

The following year at Portsmouth the fraternal greetings from the Labour Party were delivered by none other than the Prime Minister himself. In silence the delegates listened to Harold Wilson's anodyne forecast for the economy and his commitment to keeping wage increases in line with improvements in productivity. He made it clear that the Government expected the General Council to deal with unnecessary stoppages of work. This was probably a reference to the decisions of an emergency meeting of Congress held at Croydon earlier in the year which gave the General Council authority to intervene in industrial activity of individual unions both in case of inter-union disputes and normal disputes between unions and employers.

But once again the big debate at Portsmouth was on a DATA motion amended by the National Union of Sheetmetal Workers. Moved by George Doughty the motion called on Congress to reaffirm its opposition to anti-trade union legislation and other forms of interference in trade union affairs. It demanded the repeal of the Prices and Incomes Act of 1966 and required the General Council to lead affiliated unions in "aggressive opposition" until this aim was achieved. The restrictive legislation against unions "is not because of strikes" he told Congress. "The real motive comes from strains and conflicts inevitably arising from the imbalance of power and wealth between the owners and producers of wealth". On behalf of the General Council Vic Feather, TUC Secretary, argued that if the motion was passed it would leave the Council no room to manoeuvre in talks arranged with Barbara Castle. The delegates were obviously divided but carried the motion with a majority of 500,000.

In the summer of 1970 Labour's economic policies became redundant. The Tories had been elected and were talking industrial relations legislation. DATA showed strongly among the massive trade union campaign against the ill-conceived Industrial Relations Act. The General Election sprung by Edward Heath in February 1974 resulted in the return of a minority Labour Government. Nevertheless, in the seven months of its existence the Industrial Relations Act was repealed, the Pay Board abolished and the three-day week imposed by the Tory Government was terminated. As he had done in 1966 Harold Wilson decided to ask the electorate once again to give him a working majority so that Labour's manifesto promises could be carried out. Another General Election was called for October. Wilson was counting on the support of a united TUC. A great deal of political attention would be concentrated on the 106th annual Trade Union Congress to be held in Brighton in September.

Still in the honeymoon period of the amalgamation the AUEW was the acknowledged leader of left wing influence in the TUC. It was therefore not surprising that motion 49 on the congress agenda should have sent ripples of unease through the assembled delegations. It was a comprehensive motion in the name of the AUEW's Technical Administrative and Supervisory Section. It said, Congress, while recognising the evils of inflation, rejects the theory that wage rises are a major contributory factor. It therefore declares that a "social compact" can only be accepted by trade unionists when substantial progress had been made on the items which comprise an "alternative strategy" agreed by the TUC Labour Party Liaison Committee.

These were: **1.** A large scale redistribution of income and wealth; **2.** A massive increase in house building with the emphasis on homes for those in need and those on lower incomes; **3.** Municipalisation of rented property; **4.** Public ownership of land required for the housing programme; **5.** A wide ranging permanent system of price control; **6.** Vastly improved social services by the injection of necessary resources; **7.** Substantial increase in public ownership and public enterprise, coupled with public supervision of investment policies of large private corporations; **8.** Substantial cuts in defence expenditure in order to release resources to help carry through this programme.

All this was a direct challenge to the General Council whose conditions for a "Social Contract" included an undertaking that unions would voluntarily restrict wage claims to the level of the retail price index and maintain a twelve month interval between claims. In presenting the General Council's Report, Len Murray, TUC General Secretary, defended the right of unions to bargain on behalf of their members. "We reject statutory incomes policy or attempts by any institution including the TUC to impose a rigid centralised framework on collective bargaining." He went on to emphasise that "wage restraint is not a solution for Britain's continuing economic problems." The TUC was urging negotiators to stick to its guidelines and try to reach agreements that would maintain their members' living standards. In return the government would seek to raise the incomes of pensioners and trim those of speculators in shares and land and introduce measures that would benefit the whole community.

Said Ken Gill, who moved motion 49, "With the General Council's policy, when it stands bare and unadorned, wage restraint is once again revealed." As far as TASS was concerned "Wage restraint, the kernel of the Social Contract, is a continuation of the policies which have failed and which defeated us in 1970." He continued "we do not help a Labour Government by not getting a rise at Ford's or the GEC. The millions saved by those companies are not handed to Harold Wilson to boost old age pensions."

The debate went on for two hours. Nobody was denying the validity of the TASS arguments but many were clearly unhappy with the uncompromising way they were presented. Judgments were being made on how the outcome of this debate might affect Labour's changes in the forthcoming election. Lawrence Daly of the National Union of Mineworkers presented the resolutions that backed the General Council's report. Of the fourteen speakers who took part in the debate only W Kendall of the Civil and Public Services Association and W Ronksley of the Associated Society of Locomotive Engineers and Firemen said they would be supporting the TASS motion. It was obvious that Hugh Scanlon had intended to stay out of this debate. Representing the second largest union in the TUC he was now facing a dilemma. The way things were going not to speak at all would look like a cop out, yet it would be inappropriate to criticise or oppose in public a brother from his own amalgamated union. But equally he was anxious to demonstrate that the Labour Party had the united support of the TUC. In the end he decided to make a statement.

By brooding over the issues that had been aired by all the participants he avoided coming down on either side. He wondered if the employers or the CBI were going to honour the contract in the

STRIKING FASHION SENSE... Picketing workers at the gates of the Aluminium Wire and Cable Co Ltd in South Wales, February 1970, display a remarkable range of dress styles.

way he had no doubt the Labour Party and the unions would. He thought it was a pity that the debate had to take place at all. No one knew whether there would be a Labour Government or not. He seemed to agree with everything that had been said including the points advanced by Ken Gill: "When we have them (a Labour Government) returned that would be the time to have the type of debates that we are having now."

In his wind-up statement Len Murray appealed to Ken Gill to withdraw his motion. "I will give you an assurance on behalf of the General Council (I have not consulted them - they can impeach me if they like, afterwards)" he said "that those eight points will be embodied in the policies which we shall pursue with this Government." At this point the President of Congress, Lord Allen CBE asked the delegates if they wanted a five-minute recess before the vote was taken so that some delegations could make up their mind. There was no consensus in favour of an adjournment. Some delegates and the TV audience saw the finger-wagging exchange that took place between Ken Gill and Hugh Scanlon at the back of the hall. The vote on the motions that supported the General Council's report was taken and they were carried. Then the President said "I now come to motion 49. I gather the mover wishes to respond to the request made to him." Making it clear that without retracting any of its views, without retracting any of its reservations, in the interests of unity TASS would withdraw no. 49. "I have a feeling that our unity is stretched to its absolute utmost" said Ken Gill "and we shall have to refrain from supporting the actual document but we shall not be voting against it." The President thanked him for "that helpful intervention."

At the 1975 Congress the General Council continued to express support for the notion of a social contract between the trade union movement and the Labour Government. This time it took the form of a voluntary imposed £6 per week limit on pay increases, the brainchild of the highly respected leftwinger and leader of the Transport and General Workers' Union, Jack Jones. Once again Ken Gill went to the rostrum with a motion that cut right across the idea of unions holding back on pay claims.

Without actually using the words "I told you so" he recited the evidence to show that the promises they were given the previous year and which were used to persuade him to withdraw TASS's motion outlining an alternative economic strategy were turned into their opposites.

There was no change in the distribution of wealth, prices were still going up, unemployment was steadily increasing, the housing programme was a failure, defence spending had risen, public expenditure was slashed and still workers were being asked to reduce their living standards. This wage control, he said was "as voluntary as rape."The delegates did not see it that way. They favoured the General Council with a majority of 3.5 million votes.

To confirm that its General Secretary was expressing union policy the TASS Annual Conference of its Representative Council continued to pass motions condemning both statutory and voluntary incomes policies and reiterating its call for free collective bargaining. The position of the AUEW was less clear.

A problem arose when a majority on the Engineering Section's National Committee voted in support of the TUC/Labour economic policies. The President, Hugh Scanlon then ruled that the 52 members of the committee were now mandated for the AUEW policy-making National Conference which was to take place soon after. TASS and the Construction Engineers shouted foul and refused to go through the motions of a debate to reach a foregone conclusion.

As time went on there were unmistakable signs of unrest among the rank and file particularly in the public sector. Three years of wage restraint against rising prices, reductions in social services and unemployment approaching the two million mark was beginning to take its toll.

The delegates at the 1977 TUC translated the message from the members to the General Council - no more social contracts. The unofficial but very influential broad left campaigning body the Liaison Committee for the Defence of Trade Unions had rallied shop stewards all over the country to demand a return to free collective bargaining. Congress gave overwhelming support to TASS' motion for the alternative economic strategy which encompassed the conditions outlined in the one that it was compelled to withdraw in 1974.

The General Council was sharply divided on what steps it should take. One group, a minority in which Ken Gill was a prominent member, argued for positive trade union action would would force the Government to change course and go for a programme of investment, for jobs and improved social services. The majority believed the Government was doing the best it could and that the unions should go along with it. The outcome was some muted criticism of Government policies but no action. James Callaghan, who had followed Harold Wilson as Prime Minister, insisted that there should be a norm for pay increases.

The cold winds that heralded the winter of discontent were beginning to blow. Moderate policies would do what they always did for a Labour Government: lose it enough trade union votes to allow the Tories in. The real trouble for the movement was only beginning.

the watershed years

By 1974 the comings and the goings were beginning to gather pace. Conference said farewell to George Doughty who for twenty-four years had skillfully steered the union through the storm-tossed seas of the engineering and shipbuilding industry. He knew no loyalty but to his own class. He was a union activist with a clear vision of the way forward for the members he served. He became a divisional organiser in 1946 operating from the Birmingham office. Six years later he was elected General Secretary by the individual vote of the annual conference delegates. George Doughty was a man who was able to impose his presence on the engineering employers, in the TUC and in the Labour Party with authority based on conviction, commitment and confidence. He never lost touch with the rank and file and had a special regard for lay activists whose role he gratefully acknowledged was so vital to the success of the organisation. His retirement was marked by tributes from all parts of the industrial and political spectrum.

The 1975 Annual Conference, Ken Gill's first as General Secretary, began sadly with the delegates paying a different kind of tribute. They stood in silent memory of Arthur Housden whose death on the first day of the year ended a presidency that lasted a mere seven months. It was also the year that saw the passing of George Doughty's predecessor James Young, General Secretary of the AESD from 1945/1952.

George Doughty speaking at the TUC

With Vice President Barry Seager in the chair the 300-plus delegates had before them a 40-page comprehensive report detailing 24 major organisational changes designed to reflect the union's growth and the spread of membership.

The changes were mostly related to administrative matters. Responsibility for finance was given over to the General Secretary and the EC's Finance and General Purposes Sub-Committee. Tony Manson became the last General Treasurer. Pay-ment of unemployment benefit would be made when the State's Earnings Related Benefit came to an end. It was also agreed that the EC would have the authority to increase subscriptions in line with inflation.

The Editor's job was no longer to be held by a full-time official. Instead it would be done by a suitably qualified member of staff reporting direct to the General Secretary. Harry Smith, who had been the Editor, was redesignated a national organiser with industrial responsibilities. Five more divisional organisers were to be appointed and the EC was given the option of appointing additional officials to meet any increase in the demand for service. An important principle was introduced by Conference accepting the concept of "multi-manning." (TASS was always more interested in women's pay and conditions of employment than sexual semantics.) Multi-manning meant a reduction in the number of official locations with an increase of the number of officials in the field. The vestigial remains of the AESD and DATA were being given a decent burial.

The rites of passage were completed in 1976 when the delegates returned to Conference to approve a wholesale re-writing of the rule book. Words like "behove" were removed. (It was said that the more obscure passages in the rule book were due to it being originally written in Scots.)

The proposal that failed the previous year called for a drastic reduction in the size of the Executive. The vote in favour fell short of the two-thirds majority required for a rule change. Up until this time the Executive Committee consisted of lay representatives elected from each division. This made twenty-six in all. Then there was the President, the Vice-President, the past-President and the Women's representative - 11 lay members. (The General Treasurer had been dropped the year before.) The full-time officials who sat on the Committee were the General Secretary, his Deputy, the Assistant Secretary (Administration) and the Editor (another redundant position.) Only the lay members were entitled to vote.

Deputy General Secretary John Forrester had argued the year before that what was then a 35-strong committee was inefficient, unwieldy and costly. The proposal was to alter the basis of lay member representation from divisional to regional constituencies, plus the President, the Vice-President and Women's representative. It was further proposed that the only fulltime officials on the EC should be the General Secretary and his Deputy. The 1976 Conference provided the two-thirds majority with ease.

The union retained its twenty-six divisional councils but for electing an EC member these would be grouped regionally in Scotland, Ireland, the North East, the North West, Yorkshire and Humberside, the West Midlands, the East Midlands, the South West, South, Wales and East London. It was decided that the EC meeting normally held on Saturdays would be moved to mid-week, a sign of self-confidence and a more "professional" approach to the task of running a modern trade union.

Because of the disappearance of the Divisional EC members the Divisional Council Chairman was retitled Divisional Council President and was given some of the authority previously exercised by the EC member. Divisional councils had their own responsibilities extended. They could, for example, declare a dispute in their area official and could approve local agreements. Co- ordination between Divisional Council Presidents and the Executive Committee member took place at statutory monthly meetings.

Undoubtedly there was an element of cost cutting in these changes. The luxurious procedures and activities that were possible in a small craft-based union could not be sustained in an organisation that was catering for nearly 150,000 members throughout the white collar sector of the engineering industry. Already the high level of strike pay had been replaced with what was termed a flexible policy. The practice of paying out a specific percentage of take home pay had allowed some large employers, like GEC for instance, to estimate how much a strike was likely to cost the union and how long it would take for that cost to become painful. The union now gave members who were taking official strike action an undertaking that they would compensate them with lump sums either at intervals during the dispute or when it was over. As they were therefore not getting any strike pay they would be able on behalf of their families to claim whatever social security benefits might be available. It was a system that put an end to groups of members queuing up for clearance before coming out on strike. Eventually, the Tories countered this by deeming that all strikers were getting £12 per week from their union.

With a view to cutting financial outgoings still further it was agreed that Annual Conference itself should be scrutinised to see if there was any way its accelerating costs could be brought in line. This would have to be done without damaging the democratic procedures that gave the ordinary rank and file member the right to have a say in determining the union's policies.

In the meantime the Selection Committee was getting about the task of finding the new divisional organisers. Candidates for these positions had to agree that they would be available to work in any part of the country. The intention was to locate those selected in Scotland, Yorkshire, West Midlands, in London and the South East, areas of recruitment potential. Unexpectedly, Brian Richardson the Sheffield based official notified the EC that he had accepted a job with the Advisory Conciliation and Arbitration Service (ACAS) so as well as appointing new officials there would have to be a replacement.

For the first time the Committee went for the young blood. The first of the appointees were all under thirty-five. Rodney Tucker, who had been active in organising youth members and, subsequently, a London Divisional Council Secretary, took over the Sheffield Office. Roger Henshaw, who had been the EC member for the Gloucester Division went to North London. Charles Lomas from the Liverpool Division and an Executive Member of the Newton Constituency Labour Party was placed, after a sojourn in Nottingham, in the Birmingham Office. Andy Matson, the youngest of the four at the age of twenty-seven and who had been active in Clydeside from his apprenticeship days, was located in Manchester.

Early in 1976 three more divisional organisers were posted to the regions where it was reckoned there were large groups of unorganised technical and clerical staff. Barbara Switzer, the women's representative on the EC, became the first woman to fill one of these positions. She joined Roger Henshaw at the North London office. Ian Benson multimanned with Charles Lomas and John Rowan in Birmingham (from where William Shields had transferred to Glasgow). The other new organiser was Derek Perkins, an activist in the Midlands who was teamed up with Len Formby and Dick Woolf in the newly acquired offices in Richmond Surrey. Later in the year L Brooke and B King were added to the list. TASS, at the end of 1976, had 34 officials in the regions and six at headquarters. The membership had gone over 160,000.

In May that year the Annual Conference received a report dealing with the need to reform its own constitution and procedures. Besides the problem of its high cost the report pointed out that the size of the assembly and the weight of the agenda was becoming a cumbersome instrument for the resolution of union policies. The views of the membership were sought by publishing the main sections of the report in the Journal. What was needed was a means of reducing the one delegate per branch complement and a procedure for filtering motions before they arrived on the floor of the national conference.

With virtually no opposition and a relatively

modest crop of amendments the delegates in 1977 accepted thirteen proposals for the reconstitution of their annual policy-making conference. The principal innovation was the establishment of annual divisional conferences. These were a kind of mini-national conference. They consisted of elected branch delegates who would debate motions submitted by the various branches in the divisions and then select what they considered to be the best four for sending up to national level. On the basis of one per 1,750 members they would elect the delegates who would attend the representative council. The aim was to bring the number of national conference delegates down to about 100 and have a much more pertinent agenda. Another proposal was that divisional organisers, who in the days of the AESD and DATA rarely missed the opportunity of making intervention in conference debates, should no longer be required to attend. All the changes were aimed at streamlining conference procedures, allowing more time for debates and achieving what was most unusual, a completed agenda.

After sixty years the union had reached the turning point in its history. From the middle seventies the image of a rather exclusive, compact organisation concentrating its hegemony in a specific field of the engineering industry was undergoing a transformation. TASS was gearing up to extend its influence to push its boundaries wider and deeper. Big was not only beautiful, big was powerful.

The promise of one union for engineering held out by the amalgamation at the start of the decade turned out to be an industrial mirage. Everyone could see it but no one knew how to reach it. The developments in TASS in terms of organisation, structure and potentiality were in the eyes of its leadership the logical course for a union that aimed at establishing an effective presence in the only expanding sector of the industry. This naked fact of industrial life was something the manual sections could not live with. Once incompatibility had manifested itself TASS was left with no option but to pursue its own logic.

The engineering industry was undergoing its own metamorphosis. Company mergers were bringing about the ascendancy of the giant corporations, combines and conglomerates. Managerial decisions were controlled from national, international and transnational board rooms. Industrial and economic power was concentrated in fewer and fewer centres. And it was in these kind of companies that more and more TASS members were employed. "Rationalisation" had become the vogue word in trendy management circles. For TASS this meant raising its sights and focusing on the combines.

The process began in 1977 by allocating certain divisional organisers to particular industries. John Rowan looked after Leyland Cars, Joseph Lucas and Dunlop. John Tuchfeld took responsibility for Fords, General Motors, Plessey, STC, Phillips and Thorne. Shipbuilding, Aerospace and Rolls-Royce were committed to William Niven. Located respectively in multi-manned offices at Birmingham, Bushey and Richmond they did not have to report to Divisional Councils but to the EC direct. They were given the title National Industrial Officer (NIO). The mould for the future structure of the union had now been formed.

During the year two of the union's longest serving officials retired. Dick Woolf as EC member of the AESD and Divisional Organiser of DATA and TASS had been a key figure in winning support for the progressive policies that had fuelled the development of the organisation. The other was Bob Dickinson whose full-time career began when he was appointed Divisional Organiser in 1947 and which progressed to his becoming Assistant General Secretary in 1956.

Eric Winterbottom, the North London based Divisional Organiser was selected to succeed Bob Dickinson in the post now designated Assistant Secretary (Administration) and Chris Darke replaced Dick Woolf.

From 1977 into the eighties the union went through a period when officials and positions were undergoing wholesale relocation and reidentification. Much of this was due to the closures of single-official offices and the placing of officials in new multi-manned premises. Much was also due to retirements, resignations, requests for transfers and to one untimely death. In September 1978 after a brief illness John Forrester, the Deputy General Secretary died. John began his union activity in Clydeside and in 1951 became a Divisional Organiser operating from the Manchester office. He played a prominent role in the wider movement. In 1971 he was elected to the NEC of the Labour Party. He was noted for his enthusiastic campaigning in the international field, playing a leading role in the Peace Movement, on the National Committee of the Anti-Apartheid Movement and on the Executive of the Chile Solidarity Campaign. When he became Deputy General Secretary in 1974 he took part with Ken Gill in many of the tedious discussions with the Engineering Section over the form and development of the amalgamation. TASS had lost one of its outstanding officials.

Eric Winterbottom was chosen to fill the post of Deputy General Secretary and John Tuchfeld became Assistant Secretary (Administration). Additional officials and the filling of consequential vacancies resulted in the appointment of F Hyde for the Leicester Office, R Parsons to Birmingham, B Sanderson to Richmond, J Thomas to Bushey, D Yeomans to Bristol and J Simmons to Middlesborough. The retirement of such long-standing and influential officials as Harry Smith the National Organiser, Archie McAlpine, Glasgow, G Strattan, Liverpool and the resignation of F Ticehurst, Bristol, presented opportunities for divisional organisers to take up the EC's offer to consider requests for transfers before allocating those newly appointed. There were a number received, a number acceded to and a number rejected. Ron Longworth went to Wales in the trail of John Jones who asked to be posted to Bristol. J MacConnachie who had already transferred to Glasgow from Leicester was followed by Tony Foley, replacing Archie McAlpine. Charles Lomas returned to his heartland, Liverpool as the successor to George Strattan. Denis Blockley went to Ipswich and M Sourani joined the Birmingham group. Roger Henshaw left Bushey for Manchester. The three National Industrial Officers were not overlooked. Barbara Switzer moved into the position vacated by John Tuchfeld.

With regret the EC accepted John Rowan's personal reasons for wanting to be relieved of national responsibilities and allowed him to return to the ranks of the divisional organisers. As a result the Selection Committee chose Jack Carr to replace him.

John Jones found himself on the move once again when he was selected to take the National Organiser's job from which Harry Smith had retired. Now a new list of names was appearing in the divisions. Nick Burden and Bob Elliott went to Bushey, Stan Martin to Richmond, Arnold Bashforth to Birmingham and following the resignation of Don Carr, Nick Burden was posted to the Bristol office and Howell John to Bushey.

Organisational changes were taking place at a rate that would have appalled the pioneers of the union. In the matter of a few years the internal machinery had been shifted up a couple of gears and there was still a hungry look in the eyes of the leadership. The 1980 Conference had agreed to a further restructuring of the Head Office organisation. The success of the National Industrial Organisers in getting to grips with the problems posed by combines and multi-nationals led to them becoming National Organisers. The existing National Organisers were retitled Assistant Secretaries. Not surprisingly the incumbents in all these positions were confirmed in the newly created offices.

Across the Irish Sea the members who fifteen years ago could only call on one official based in Liverpool had their own organisers in Belfast and Dublin offices. In 1978 Brian Graham and Brian Anderson produced a joint report on how they saw the membership in Ireland developing. In this they were optimistic enough to anticipate the need for another divisional organiser, possibly in Cork. Joe Bowers, the Irish EC member was selected to take over the Belfast office on the retirement of Brian Graham in 1981 and in 1983 Gerry Shanahan became the third Irish Divisional Organiser, but in Dublin not Cork.

It would have been too much to expect such changes not to effect some of the personnel concerned. The EC in consultation with the representatives of the full-time officers devised a procedure whereby any grievances felt by either party could be dealt with on a formal basis should the normal informal "talking it over" fail to resolve the problem.

At the 1980 Recall Conference at which the legal issues regarding the amalgamation were being discussed the EC took the opportunity of acquainting the assembled delegates with the terms of the proposed procedure. The delegates saw the point and gave it their overwhelming approval. In two cases it had to be used. One occurred in 1982 when extensive discussions having failed to settle his disagreements with lay activists Ian Benson, the Divisional Organiser for East London, resigned. Again in 1983 the Glasgow based Divisional Organiser, J MacConnachie, following a row with certain members of his Divisional Council, found it impossible to cope with the transfer to Durham proposed by the EC. He also resigned.

In 1983 personal differences compelled the EC to accept the resignation of National Organiser W Niven. After indicating he was not in a position to accept a transfer from Birmingham to London A Bashforth gave in his resignation in 1983.

With the transfer of engagements of the National Union of Gold Silver and Allied Trades into TASS the officials of that union had to be accommodated. The outcome was Brian Bridges after a spell in Sheffield was allocated to the South London office and given national responsibilities. Bryn Waters took over in Cardiff. The significance of the connection with NUGSAT was that it showed how other unions could be fitted without loss of identity into the TASS organisation. This experience was an important influence in the discussions that were beginning with the Sheet Metal Workers, the Pattern Makers and the Metal Mechanics.

The restructuring and re-organisation of TASS had proceeded while the grand plan for the establishing of one big union for all classes of employees in the engineering industry was being demolished. It was as if TASS had been laying the table for a banquet but because those invited did not like the seating arrangements they refused to come. So rather than discard preparations TASS went out into the highways and byways of the industry and found those who were more than willing to join its company. The gathering that transpired was probably better than the one that was intended.

David Kitson: a case of solidarity

A sore point with the left wing of the AESD was its failure in 1953 to prevent £1,153 of the Association's funds being invested in South African stock. Five years later the issue was raised again in a motion from the Chelmsford Branch which urged that the investment should be withdrawn. An amendment from Hatfield added that the TUC should be asked to advise any union with funds invested in South Africa to do likewise.

The debate was along the battlelines drawn between the left and right wing factions - a trial of strength. The Executive Committee opposed the motion and the amendment on the grounds that it was up to other unions to make their own decisions and that approval or disapproval of political regimes should not influence the Association's investment programme.

Mr R Huzzard from the Mayfair Branch pointed out to delegates that the South African Government with its institutionalised racial discrimination and rejection of democratic trade unionism was unique and not at all comparable with any other political system. The motion as amended was carried. The Association withdrew its money from the South African stock and the TUC when approached about other unions' investments was able to inform the EC that as far as it was aware no other union had put money in South Africa.

From time to time articles appeared in the "Draughtsman" describing the brutalities and injustices to black people under the rule of the white minority in South Africa. At almost every annual conference there was bound to be a statement on the plight of these black workers. It could be said that representatives of the Association were sure to be found in the ranks of any anti-apartheid demonstration.

In the August 1964 edition of the "Draughtsman" there appeared a brief paragraph from the EC Report. It merely stated that "Information had been received" that a member of DATA who returned to South Africa about three years ago had been arrested, held in solitary confinement and without trial under the notorious "ninety-day" law. It went on to describe Mr Kitson's active involvement with the Association as an annual conference delegate and as a holder of a DATA scholarship at Ruskin College, Oxford. DATA was making the strongest possible protest to the South African Government.

While the EC was telling the South African Government that David Kitson should either be charged and tried or set free, a group of London-based members had formed a committee to organise a "Release David Kitson" campaign.

In South Africa, David's wife Norma was publicising the harsh brutalities her husband was suffer-

David Kitson

ing at the hand of the police authorities. She infuriated the Government by standing on the steps of Johannes-burg City Hall with her two children, Steven aged seven and Amanda aged two, demanding in public that her husband be charged or released. Because she was kicking up such a fuss she was herself arrested and thrown into gaol, without being charged and detained for four weeks. An interview she had previously given to a Sunday Times of South Africa reporter was widely circulated in Britain and may have been a factor which led to her regaining her freedom.

The DATA-organised campaign of demonstrations, marches and publicity began with a Trade Union and Labour Movement rally in Hyde Park followed by a poster parade through the West End and culminating in an all-night vigil outside South Africa House in Trafalgar Square. Through its international affiliations DATA was able to call upon the support of the European white collar trade unions in further protest to the South African Government. The DATA Journal urged all its readers to write to the South African Ambassador in London and to David Kitson in Pretoria Prison. Similar letters were sent to the major TUC unions.

Norma Kitson was given only a few days' notice that she would have to find the money to pay for the defence of her husband who was being brought to trial on 18 November 1964. The DATA Executive Committee immediately gave an undertaking to give all the help it could and launched an appeal throughout the movement and its own membership for voluntary donations.

By March 1965 over £3,000 had been collected and over £2,000 of this had been used towards the legal costs. The outcome of the trial was that David Kitson and two colleagues were sentenced to twenty years imprisonment. They were found guilty of being involved in an armed struggle against apartheid at the time when the South African Government had made peaceful protest illegal.

At the 1965 Annual Conference DATA President, Archie McAlpine pledged the Association's continued support for Norma Kitson and her children. Just before he was sentenced David Kitson managed to get a letter through to a friend in England. In it he said that even in solitary confinement he had an inkling of the efforts the union was making on his behalf. It helped to uplift his moral. "What made me grateful and proud to be a member of DATA is to read of the scale of your support for me."

There was no let-up in this support for the whole term of David Kitson's imprisonment. Such was the enthusiasm and energy put into the campaign by the London Divisional Council members who made up the "Kitson Committee" that his cause was carried from there into the mainstream of DATA activity. It was funded by voluntary donations and from collections and special functions arranged to publicise and stimulate interest as widely as possible.

It was as a result of the committee's initiative that each year sacks of Christmas cards from DATA members for David Kitson were piled up in the stores of Pretoria Prison. National officials led powerful delegations to the Foreign Office, to lobby MPs at Parliament and to South Africa House pressing all the time for the South African Government to release David Kitson and allow him to return to Britain.

Due to the difficulties she was experiencing in

trying to live in South Africa Norma Kitson decided in 1966 to come back to England. An EC decision to provide £1,600 towards the purchase of a flat in the London area and to act as guarantor for a mortgage of £4,000 for the Kitson family was agreed at the union's annual conference. Money was also sent to South Africa to cover education fees for studies Dave Kitson was undertaking in prison. Unfortunately, a number of years went by without the union hearing anything from the family.

DATA, however, maintained its untiring efforts to keep the plight of David before the membership and used every opportunity to involve national and international institutions in raising the issue at home and abroad. Through an extremely active Kitson Committee at Ruskin College the demonstrations, protest marches and fund-raising functions never flagged. The DATA sponsorship to Ruskin was renamed David Kitson Scholarship.

In 1970 it was as a result of continuing pressure of this nature that David Kitson was give the status of 'A' grade prisoner. This meant two visits per month, permission to buy food and three letters per month. Welcome as this development was, the DATA campaign was about getting David Kitson released. And so it went on year after year, keeping the membership informed with regular bulletins, articles and special events ensuring that interest in David would be sustained.

Indeed, so much was the David Kitson Campaign an intrinsic feature of the DATA organisation that some members wrote letters to the Journal complaining about the amount of time and money wasted on someone who had been tried and found guilty of a criminal offence.

Significantly, when the Editor or a member of the Kitson Committee replied to the letters those who had written them almost invariably withdrew their complaints or conceded that they had not been aware of all the facts when they wrote.

The Kitson Committee stall with its leaflets, posters, badges and collecting boxes was a regular feature at the union's annual conference, as was the Kitson Evening Meeting which was addressed by either prominent Anti- Apartheid speakers or ex-prisoners of the South African Government or representatives of the African National Congress.

As the long years rolled on the DATA and in the seventies the TASS campaign for the release of David Kitson never let up. Every possible and some improbable strings were pulled. No opportunity of raising the issue was missed including making direct representations to the Foreign Office whether there was a Labour or Tory administration.

It was, however, in 1974 that in a meeting with the then Foreign Secretary, Anthony Crosland, the idea was floated that it might be possible to arrange a post for David Kitson at Ruskin College, Oxford, if he were freed. Crosland felt this was a strong negotiating factor in as much as it could convince the South African Authorities that once he was out of gaol David Kitson would be returning to England. Unfortunately, the sudden death of Anthony Crosland prevented any further progress being made along these lines.

Nevertheless, the political pressure was kept up. David Owen, who succeeded Crosland, undertook to raise the case with the South African Government and accepted a petition organised by the Ruskin students that gathered 18,500 signatures. Into the 1980s a similar undertaking was given by the Tory Under-Secretary for South African Affairs, Richard Luce, who went as far as making a public statement in support of David and to press for study rights for political prisoners. Right up to his release in 1984 the union's campaign never lost its impetus:

Des Starrs, Chairman of the London based Kitson Committee

a remarkable feat by any standards but all the more so because it was due entirely to the commitment and dedication of ordinary lay members. While the full-time officers used their position and authority to back up the various activities, the donkey work was being done by the lay members of the London and Ruskin-based Kitson Committees. It would be impracticable and invidious to attempt a list of all those who contributed to keeping the Kitson issue alive. But many of them would want to record the outstanding role played by Des Starrs, the Chairman of the London-based Kitson Committee.

When David Kitson returned to England the union in co-operation with the ANC arranged a countrywide lecture tour to major centres. The intention was to provide David with an opportunity of recounting to as wide an audience as possible his experiences as a white prisoner of a racist regime. Regional officials of the union prepared media packs to ensure the widest publicity for the lectures and concentrated on getting a large turnout of Labour Party and trade union members. The tour was a great success.

Yet the union's activity on behalf of David Kitson was but part of its declared support for the Anti Apartheid Movement. DATA had urged the Labour Government in 1965 to back the UN sanctions against South Africa.

When in 1971 the Tory Government decided to permit the sale of arms to South Africa the DATA EC was instructed by Annual Conference to officially support any workers who refused to work on South African arms contracts. It was in 1972 the union formally affiliated to the Anti-Apartheid Movement.

The Tobacco Workers Union and TASS jointly persuaded the TUC in 1976 to carry a motion calling for an end to all British investment in South Africa, an arms embargo and support for the African liberation movement. TASS has also for many years expressed its support for the South African Black trade unions congress, SACTU and in 1980 Ken Gill became the first ever member of the General Council to speak on behalf of the TUC on a SACTU platform.

On his release in 1984, to help David get settled TASS decided to activate the suggestion it had made to Anthony Crosland in 1974. An agreement was negotiated with the Ruskin College Authorities in which TASS undertook to sponsor a lectureship for David at a salary of £12,000 per annum. Obviously this commitment had to take into consideration the fact that he was approaching the retiral age for a Ruskin Fellowship. A lifetime guarantee of sponsorship would have been inappropriate.

Regrettably, things did not turn out as might have been expected. The Kitson family were prominent members of the London City Group of the Anti-Apartheid Movement. This organisation was opposed to the strategy of the national body. The Group's aim was to compel the AAM to attack racism everywhere.

Not only did the London Group publicly attack and disparage the national Anti-Apartheid policy it also alarmingly launched out against the African National Congress which had always been given the full support of the union. In the eyes of the AAM David Kitson had aligned himself with those who were creating disruption and diversion within the Movement. The great majority of Anti-Apartheid activists were extremely angry at the creation of dissension just at a time when, due to the urgency of the political situation in South Africa, the maximum unity was of vital importance. In the light of this experience the ANC suspended David Kitson from membership.

At the 1986 Annual Conference David Kitson revealed his hand when as a delegate he moved an amendment that was intended to commit the union to the support of liberation forces other than the African National Congress. This was principally to support the Pan African Congress, an ultra-left black consciousness movement.

The overwhelming majority of delegates were shocked at the idea that someone who had suffered twenty years imprisonment for supporting the ANC should now seek to diminish its leading role in the fight against apartheid. They rejected the amendment.

In the end the union decided it could no longer sponsor a member who was actively campaigning against its policies and who was in dispute with the movement that for years it had promoted and assisted. To compensate for any financial difficulties that might have arisen from this decision and in recognition of his past services the union offered David a year's salary.

It did not take David's family and their supporters long to mount a campaign in TASS and in the broader movement attacking the union and its leadership. They complained that TASS was undermining academic freedom by withdrawing its sponsorship from a member who disagreed with its policies. They also insisted that the union had promised to fund David for life, even though no official or active member have ever sought or been granted such a condition. As was mentioned above, the arrangements with Ruskin had in mind that David Kitson reached retirement age in 1984 and would, therefore, have been in line with the perceptions of the general membership.

The union's record on how it responded to the plight of David Kitson and his family from the time of his arrest in 1964 stands open to fair scrutiny. There was in the end a feeling of great disappointment that after all that an attempt should be made to use it as a fig leaf to give respectability to political groups set on spreading division in the labour and trade union movement.

the "Confed"

The AESD, in its early days, participated with other non-manual unions in the Engineering and Shipbuilding Staff Workers' Alliance. This was eventually replaced by the Joint Consultative Committee of Staff Unions, a body with executive authority operating under the umbrella of the Confederation of Shipbuilding and Engineering Unions. In 1943 the draughtsmen decided to fully affiliate to the "Confed" as it was known. Needless to say, there were those voices that warned about the loss of independence and being swept into manual workers' disputes. More progressive voices were able to give assurance that there was no question of the Association losing its autonomy. Affiliating to the CSEU was seen as a logical step following the decision to go for a national wage agreement with the Engineering Employers' Federation. It also gave the draughtsmen an opportunity of having representatives on shop stewards' and CSEU District Committees. The main concern of the Confederation was issues affecting manual workers; in 1960 for instance only five out of its forty affiliates represented staff workers. It was also dominated by the Amalgamated Engineering Union with the largest membership in the industry.

Back in 1933 the AESD and the AEU had raised at the TUC Annual Conference the question of the "socialisation" of the engineering industry. The TUC accepted a memorandum on the subject but then buried it. It was 1951 before it was brought up again.

This time the call for the extension of public ownership and the setting up of Development Council was expressed in the CSEU Policy Document "The Plan for Engineering". The AESD had been responsible for most of the content of this detailed examination into the needs of the different sections of the industry. The aim was to canvass support for the plan and in co-operation with the TUC push it on to the political agenda. It was due to the efforts of the Association's representatives that for many years the Plan for Engineering was kept alive at CSEU and TUC Conferences. What the unions were proposing was rationalisation and the planned development of mutually supportive production units with procedures to involve the workers in the decision making processes. What actually happened was a series of takeovers and mergers that allowed the transnational and national combines run by accountants to move in. Technological innovation was directed towards cost cutting and profit building. Rationalisation meant the sack for thousands of workers. Governments acted negatively or not at all. The CSEU's aspirations, despite the validity of their arguments, faded into the mists of trade union lost causes. When Rolls-Royce, Leyland Motors, shipbuilding, aircraft manufacturing and steel were nationalised it had nothing to do with socialist economics: it was the tax payer picking up the tabs for the private owners' liabilities brought about by neglect or avarice.

It was the soundly reasoned and articulately expressed contributions from DATA delegations, led throughout the sixties by George Doughty and Jim Mortimer that gained the Association its high standing in the Councils of the CSEU. In 1962 George Doughty became the first non-manual leader to be elected President. On completion of his term of office he occupied the position of Trustee. Jim Mortimer did a stint on the Standing Orders Committee. When the TUC requested a nomination from the CSEU for the Mechanical Engineering Advisory Committee to the 1964 National Economic Development Council, George Doughty's name was put forward. He was at the time abroad on union business. When he returned to this country and was told of the nomination he immediately informed the Confederation that he was not prepared to act on such a Committee. It was not in his opinion, what it appeared to be and besides his union had expressed its opposition to the whole NEDDY concept. The CSEU Executive Council agreed to withdraw the nomination.

With the bulk of its affiliated membership in the area of industrial production the Confederation possessed, in the eyes of DATA activists, the potential for becoming a powerful political and industrial pressure group that could be won through control of working class institutions. During the sixties and seventies the trade union scene was a battleground for conflicting ideologies. The significance of the struggle between left and right in the CSEU lay in the effect its outcome would have on the policies of the TUC and ultimately on the Labour Party. Lining up with the left, DATA supported and projected motions that reflected its own conference decisions - against any form of wage control, against the Common Market, for full employment, for better occupational health services, against trade union legislation, for shorter working hours and for improved rates of pay. With regard to engineering itself DATA, besides keeping alive the "Plan for Engineering", laid particular emphasis on the needs of the aircraft industry for which its leading representatives were the acknowledged spokesmen.

When the Government appointed Committee of Enquiry into Engineering Design, under the Chairmanship of Professor Frank Fielden, published its report in late 1963 DATA seized upon its findings as a justification for its policy of driving up the wages of its technician members. It also made sure that the "Confed" was fully behind the recommendations of the report.

Once DATA became the Technical, Administrative and Supervisory Section of the AUEW the expectations were for an enhanced influence on CSEU policies and the establishment of a foundation upon which an effective relationship between blue and white collar workers could be built.

The CSEU claim in 1973 for an increase in the skilled workers' minimum time rate to £35 per week, the introduction of the 35-hour week and improved holidays without loss of pay, met with what trade unionists refer to as a derisory response. TASS had a parallel claim in the hands of the Engineering Employers' Federation and had no kind of a response. When the manual workers agreed to operate an overtime ban TASS urged its members to go along with them. In the main they did. Certainly there were no reports of TASS members doing anything to help out employers who were moaning about the adverse effects of the overtime ban. About five months after the claim was presented the CSEU negotiators got around the table with those of the EEF. The meeting was prompted by the intervention of the Secretary of State for Employment, TASS member Albert Booth. The employers increased their original offer of £2.50 per week to £3.50 with an additional three days holiday to bring the entitlement up to four weeks. The unions settled. Nothing came of the TASS claim. The employers' rejection was couched in terms that indicated they would no longer be interested in national wage agreements. TASS members were informed that as this was the case the procedure covering the stages through which claims were taken would terminate at Works Conference level, when the matter had been dealt with by the appropriate full-time official.

During the second half of the seventies despite the problems arising from the deteriorating relationships within the AUEW, TASS along with the other affiliates was involved in the CSEU campaign to halt the serious decline in the manufacturing sector of the economy. Important political and industrial decisions would have to be taken in a situation where companies were closing down and unemployment steadily rising. The plans to nationalise the shipbuilding and areospace industries were running into difficulties. The unions wanted to talk about industrial democracy and centralised bargaining arrangements. The employers were talking cutbacks and redundancies.

There was also the problem arising from some local managers, principally in the aerospace industry, encouraging the introduction and formation of quasi unions and staff associations. With TASS well to the fore the "Confed" let it be know that it would not tolerate moves that would lead to the proliferation of organisations in industries where already there were enough traditional unions to cater for employees at every level. TASS activists were particularly conscious of the fact that organisations such as the Shipbuilding and Aerospace Industries Management Association and the Engineering Management Association would be unviable if they were to restrict their recruitment activities to those staff sectors indicated in their titles. Were they to succeed in getting a foothold in the industries they would make a pitch for certain staff employees in any category who wanted the advantages of trade union negotiations while distancing themselves from the working class movement. They did not succeed.

Due to the concentration of members in shipbuilding, aircraft manufacture and car making TASS had always been a high profile lobbyist for Government intervention in support for these particular industries.

It had always been the policy of DATA and TASS to give its industrial and political support to the CSEU campaigns against both Tory and Labour Governments which for instance seemed to be bent on cancelling British aircraft projects and increasing reliance on American manufacturers. In the case of shipbuilding, after suffering years of stagnation due to lack of investment under private ownership, the nationalised British Shipbuilders found itself forced to compete for orders against the highly subsidised overseas yards. Here again the unions lobbied and urged Governments to up their commitment to expand and modernise the industry. They met with little success.

When the Thatcher administration came into power not only were the Engineering Unions faced with the deterioration of the British manufacturing sector but they were also subjected to trade union legislation that undermined the members' bargaining power and made demonstrations of solidarity illegal.

Following the retirement of George Doughty in 1974 Ken Gill was elected to the Executive Council of the CSEU. He later became a Trustee and a member of the General Purposes Committee, the Shipyard Negotiating Sub-Committee and until 1982 he chaired the Aerospace Sub-Committee. TASS Deputy General Secretaries Eric Winterbottom and his successor Barbara Switzer were also elected to the Executive Council.

Both played a prominent role in the Recruitment, Training and Re-training Sub-Committee and occasionally substituted for the General Secretary when he was elected to the Power Manufacturing Sub-Committee. TASS was not inclined to hide its light under a bushel. Its motivation was to project its policies into the wider movement and join with other unions in the struggle to preserve jobs in what it saw as key manufacturing industries.

Leaving aside self interest the union had always held that a Government would only be able to build prosperity for the whole nation from a strong manufacturing base. It was ironic that other industrial nations were very evidently aware of this fact. Britain, once the workshop of the world, a reservoir of craft skills and inventiveness, opted for diminishing and narrowing its technological inheritance.

women make their mark

Although the physical demands of the job were minimal draughtsmanship was considered to be a male occupation. This was probably due to the fact that the traditional route to the drawing office was via the engineering workshop. Socialising influences tended to disassociate women from an industry involving noisy machinery and dirty hands. Not that the same argument would be upheld in the textile industries or in times of war. In most major engineering and shipbuilding companies draughtsmen were recruited from craft apprentices who were ambitious. In social class terms gaining a position in the company drawing office was seen as upward mobility. Some women succeeded in overcoming this cultural barrier, but they were few and far between.

In drawing offices women were used exclusively as tracers. To preserve and store the rather fragile drawings made by draughtsmen it was necessary to have them traced on to a prepared linen-based material. It was a job that called for neat linework and lettering, not to mention good eyesight.

When the AESD was founded, tracers did not qualify for membership. Some joined a clerical workers' union but most were unorganised. In 1919 the AESD showed interest in a report that tracers were going to try to form their own union. The Tracers' Association which resulted only lasted two years. With 600 paying members it was found to be unviable. Having been approached with a view to an amalgamation the Draughtsmen's Association agreed at its 1922 Conference to establish a section to which the members of the now dissolved Tracers' Association could apply. Initially, only 200 did. In 1923 the AESD formed a National Tracers' Sub-Committee and provision was made for direct tracer representation on the Executive Committee. In the same year the Association achieved negotiating rights for tracers within the terms of its first national procedure agreement.

Persuading tracers to join the union was not easy: something the engineering employers may have taken into account when they conceded negotiating rights without demur. The fact was that the majority of women workers and especially those in office jobs could not see any benefit in joining male dominated trade unions. The left-leaning politics of the AESD and later DATA, meant that they had a better record in providing services for women members than most craft based unions. Besides having tracers' committees at divisional and national level, efforts were made to ensure that the Association was represented on those bodies which dealt with matters related to the conditions of working women, such as the TUC Women's Conference and the Women's Labour Party Conference. Yet in spite of all this the problem of recruiting women members remained. For one thing the pool from which potential members might be drawn was a tiny proportion of the female workforce. Draughtswomen or female technicians were such rarities that the union would have had to organise search parties to find them. It was hoped that the change from the AESD to DATA would alter this perspective.

It was going to take more than a change of title to overcome the cultural and social barriers that were separating women workers from effective trade unionism. Somewhere out there, a small band of committed tracers were struggling against apathy and indifference to raise the issues that might kindle a spark of interest. Their activities warranted little more than passing references in the reports of the proceedings at the Annual Conference.

A more revealing feature of the female membership showed up in the workplaces where the union organisation was strong. If a dispute took place and the decision was to take industrial action the tracers were among the first to join the picket lines. In the minimum rates and holidays campaigns which had been responsible for many of the bitterest and longest strikes in the union, the records show that the tracer members remained steadfast in their support until settlements were reached. And this was despite the enormous gap between their own minimum rates and those of the draughtsmen.

It was at the 1963 Annual Conference when DATA was two years old that a serious debate took place on the question of the tracers' organisation. The General Secretary, George Doughty, moved a report from the EC that acknowledged the hard work being done on behalf of the union by the tracers' sub-committee but expressed disappointment at how little progress was being made in improving the size of the membership. The EC had in the circumstances decided to maintain the tracers' structure "and keep under review methods by which it may be improved".

Draughtsmen were never at a loss once it was suggested that something needed improvement. Speaker after speaker rose to explain what could be done to get tracers more involved in union activity. The York branch delegate A McTurk thought the EC could in fact have done something about the voting disadvantages tracer delegates had on Divisional Councils. He moved reference back of the EC Report. In came D Starrs from Croydon Branch musing on the question of whether tracers had a separate organisational structure because they were tracers or because they were women. "Was there not" he asked "a certain amount of sentimentality in the idea of a separate structure?" This provoked a number of exchanges for and against the tracers' separate organisation. It was T McLennan from Clydebank who thought that they had all slipped up when the re-organisation was taking place. He recalled the time when there were plenty of male tracers in the industry. "Is now the time" he asked "to consider the female membership of the Association, not as tracers but as female members of it?" On behalf of the EC H Smith, a past President, acknowledged the disadvantage which women experienced in society. He argued that the existing structure offered tracers a centre in which they could get together and draw strength from each other. He asked Conference to reject the reference back and to accept the report for what it said. Conference agreed.

The Annual Conference in 1964 dealt with a motion from Birmingham North Branch that proposed the doing away with Women's Committees altogether. They led to segregation of male and female trade union members, it said. An amendment from the Bradford Branch made the motion read that "we agreed with the formation of Women's Committees as a means of expressing the points of view of women." A direct negative but nevertheless accepted and approved by the delegates. Ann McCall, the tracers' representative on the Executive Committee, agreed with the amendment pointing out that nothing could be done about the National Tracer's Sub-Committee until the next rules conference. In passing she reminded the delegates that the trade unions were a man's world and it was easier for girls to go to a tracers' meeting than to go to a branch meeting.

At last in 1966 the rules were changed. All reference to "tracer members" became simply "tracers" and the National Tracers' Sub-Committee was reconstructed as the National Women's Sub-Committee. Similarly, Divisional Womens' Sub-Committees were established and as the rules indicated all female members were now eligible to hold office in these committees. Special week- end schools were arranged for women only. DATA was represented at the Labour Womens' Conference and at the Conference of Unions catering for women workers. Then in 1967 with due formality the NWSC announced a list of matters of concern to women members.

These were: training of tracers, rates for apprentice tracers, award of a certificate on completion of training and the establishment of a scale of wages up to thirty years for tracers. Old habits, as they say, die hard.

Nothing was ever done to find out if marriage between tracers and draughtsmen was statistically interesting. There was plenty of evidence to show they shared a common interest in minimum rates. But it was not surprising that in spite of the wider remit implied by the new name of the sub-committee things carried on more or less as before. The tracers' response was the same as the draughtsmen's when the title of the Association was changed. But there were occasional signs that the process of adjustment was beginning. A few women activists were reporting their deliberations on matters concerning other workers besides tracers: equal pay, discrimination, redundancy and recruitment for instance. The main problem of getting more women involved and of making contact with the thousands of unorganised women in the engineering industry remained unresolved.

Two significant events occurred at the 1970 Annual Conference held in Blackpool. One was the arrival of a delegation from the first all-women strike in DATA. Tracers from the Plessey Company at Edge Lane, Liverpool, were out for an improved pay offer. They had made the trip to Blackpool as a morale booster and to take up a collection. They were successful on all counts. After four weeks picketing the Plessey Management caved in and conceded the increases. The second event was the unanimous acceptance by the conference delegates of a motion from Dublin, Guildford and North London Branches calling on the Executive Committee to do something about the structure and function of the Women's Committees.

Twelve months later at Eastbourne the EC announced its recommendations. First of all it agreed that the Women's Committees were not working. Therefore, its suggestion was to do away with them. In their place it recommended the setting up of Divisional Advisories and a National Women's Advisory Committee. These would meet a couple of times per year or when necessary. A further proposal was to remove the Women's representative from the Executive Committee but to allow a National Women's Advisory Committee member to be involved in all national negotiations affecting

FEMALE LEAD... March protesting at Yarrow & Co lockout. The acceptance of women within the union took time but steady progress culminated with the selection in 1983 of Barbara Switzer as Deputy General Secretary in succesion to E Winterbottom.

women. When A McTurk, who ironically had the job of presenting the report on behalf of the EC, sat down Ann Solomon, the delegate from London Central Branch, leaped to the rostrum. She accused the EC of not doing its homework.

All the signs were that women were becoming more militant and were joining unions in greater numbers than ever. The Women's Committee may not have done much in the past but they did provide a training ground for new activists. Her final thrust was to tell the EC that the employers were the only ones that would agree with its recommendations, they knew the value of keeping women in a subordinate position. She moved reference back of the report.

Bernice Tinton, a member of the National Women's Sub-Committee told the EC that it would be many years before men and women lived and worked in a truly equal society. As far as she was concerned the EC was proposing to weaken the position of women in the union and stress the leading role of the male Executive Committee. (She probably remembered the photograph in the June issue of the Journal the previous year that set out all the members of the Executive without the Women's representative.) She believed that presenting the recommendations as a part of the overall EC report to Conference was a device intended to get it pushed through. She urged the delegates to support the reference back. Ron Longworth, the delegate from West Cumberland Branch and Joe Shaw, the EC member for Scotland, exercising his right to speak as an individual member of Conference, strongly endorsed the reference back motion. Ron Longworth thought the EC recommendations were suicidal and Joe Shaw made the philosophic point that no nation could be free as long as it tolerated limited rights for half its people.

In defence of the EC A McTurk pointed out that the Women's Committees were in stagnation and were a waste of time. He insisted that all the women needed was a committee in an advisory form. The delegates thought otherwise and carried the reference back.

The EC got the message and there was no evidence that it was prepared to get burned fingers over women's representation in the union again. The 1972 Conference at Scarborough saw the emphasis moving to the broader and more reputable issue of equal pay. Mike Cooley in his Presidential address commenting on the national claim of the Confederation of Shipbuilding and Engineering Unions for equal pay for all women in the industry, reminded delegates that this was the oldest wage claim in the history of the trade union movement. "Now was the time" he said "to give full industrial vent to the pious resolutions the CSEU had been passing for the past eighty years." He went on, "women in engineering had a greater total strike power than the whole of the industrial workforce during the 1926 General Strike." DATA was launching itself into women's liberation.

This was the period when the political and industrial consciousness of the women activists began to take over from their narrow craft interests. Many of them, although still working in the tracing offices, were now addressing the big political and economic questions around the role of women in society.

Coincidental with the movement towards amalgamation there was a notable increase in the number of women activists. It was also noticeable that women who were having problems with their employers were now less inclined to look around and see if "the union", meaning the men, were going to do anything about it. Typical, were two strikes in

1973 in which women members took on employers who thought they were dealing with cheap easily exploitable labour.

In the small Yorkshire wool town of Elland women clerical workers employed by Nu-Swift International, manufacturers of fire-fighting equipment, joined TASS. They were paid very little and a condition of employment was that they should work alternate Sundays for nothing. After a lot of arguing the union persuaded the management to make an offer of a rise. It came up with a figure that fell below the restricted level of increase allowed under the Tory's Incomes Policy. The women walked out. Word came to them from the AUEW Engineering Section production workers on the shopfloor that they also were prepared to down tools until the issue was settled. Pickets were organised. Deliveries to the plant stopped. The factory ceased to function. But the management encouraged by the Engineering Employers' Association seemed determined to hold out. Press and television coverage won public support for the strikers. A delegation went to London to picket Nu-Swift Head Office. They found it boarded up and shuttered. Ted Bishop, the TASS sponsored MP and Labour's main spokesman on women's conditions of employment, undertook to raise the strike in the House of Commons. Contact was made with the Fire Brigades Union who had a special interest in the company's product. The pressures paid off. A revised offer, giving large rises all round, was put on the table. The working week was regularised, reduced to five days with overtime payment for Saturday mornings. The establishment of a joint shop stewards committee of production workers and staff meant things would never be allowed to get as bad again.

In the same year a bizzare industrial relations situation, in which women workers played the leading roles occurred at the London centre of Seiko, the Japanese owned watch manufacturer. It was a small operation consisting of ten watchmakers, plus women clerical workers and management. Every one was kept busy and there was a happy working atmosphere. No one thought there was any need to have a union. The story of how things went horribly wrong was told in the TASS Journal by Madeleine Meggs, one of the leading representatives of the clerks.

It all started with the appointment of a new under-manager who apparently believed that there was no point in managing if you cannot throw your weight about. He was particularly good at reducing the women to tears. He reckoned this was how to get the best out of them. When the happy working atmosphere had deteriorated to unmitigated misery the staff tried to complain to the powers they hoped would be; they met with the classic managerial one-liner "If you don't like it here, too bad. You know what to do." When one of the watchmakers was sacked after a row with the under-manager, what they did was join the AUEW, the men in the Engineering Section and the women in TASS. It became obvious that this management intended to have no truck with unions. And to prove this was so everybody was sacked. If they wanted their jobs back they were told they would now have to apply individually. Nobody did.

After five weeks of picketing and no sign of a settlement the workers decided drastic action was needed. One morning before the managers arrived at the offices the strikers got in. They barricaded the doors but not with any old furniture, they used cabinets containing thousands of pounds worth of delicate spare parts for watches.

There was no better way of preventing a forced entry. The police showed up and phoned in

Barbara Switzer, the first woman to hold senior office in the union.

to see if the strikers would talk to the managers. They were told that the union officials would do the talking from now on. With the press and TV recording the occupation, the under-manager who started it all busied himself by building a barricade on the outside presumably to keep the workers in. A psychiatrist would have been able to explain this behaviour. In the event negotiations were arranged for the following day with a company director who up until then had done everything he could to distance himself from the affair. After a morning of talks the union officials arrived at the offices with terms for an agreement: reinstatement of all members; complete union recognition; as a goodwill gesture, five weeks back pay; all cards stamped up to date; an agreed procedure for dealing with grievances. Both sides had learned something about workers' solidarity.

With growing confidence more and more women in the engineering industry were joining TASS and demonstrating their willingness to fight for better pay and working conditions. From about 3,000 in 1970 their membership leapt to 20,000 in 1979.

Throughout the sixties and into the seventies fundamental questions relating to the role of women in western industrialised society were being raised in public forums. The women's movement was on the march. A response to this surge of interest in the feminist cause was the fact that more women workers were joining trade unions and demonstrating their willingness to fight for better pay and conditions of employment.

DATA and then TASS which always saw itself in the van of progressive social and political movements ran the flag of women's rights to the masthead. Equal pay, equal opportunity in everything from training to promotion, maternity leave, creche facilities for working mothers, sexual discrimination and sexual harassment became the subjects of recruitment literature, weekend schools and special conferences. In 1974 Judith Hunt was appointed the union's first full-time women's officer.

This was the year acclaimed as International Women's Year. The union marked it with a press conference organised and run by women activists. Judith Hunt's booklet "Women's Rights and What We Are Doing To Get Them" was launched. The theme of the TASS campaign was expressed in the slogan "Men's Pay for Women". What it meant was that firms hiring female staff should offer pay equivalent to the rate that men would expect if they were being taken on. The TASS intention was to try and open the restrictive clauses in the Act that said women should be doing the same or broadly similar work to men in order to claim equal pay. In 1975 when the Act was implemented the number of disputes involving women increased. Most were based on a loose interpretation of the Equal Pay Act.

Helped more by the support from male trade unionists than by the legislation women members won substantial pay increases at Lyes Bronx Engineering - Stafford, Louis Newmark - Ipswich, Shaw Petrie Ltd and Cockburns Valves - Glasgow, Clarkston International Tools Ltd - Sheffield, Magnetic and Electrical Ltd - Lanarkshire and at General Electric, Liverpool. These and many more disputes involving some form of industrial action were conducted under what was assumed to be the spirit rather than the letter of the Equal Pay Act.

Unfortunately for women workers it was not long before the employers copped on that they had nothing to fear from the legislation as it stood and minor adjustments to job titles here and there were enough to shoo off any claims based on the Equal Pay Act. But the union was well used to dealing with employers who said 'no'. It did not hesitate in taking them on where the women members were willing and there was a reasonable chance of winning.

Over the period when the consciousness of women was apparently being raised, the gains in pay and conditions of employment achieved by women workers taking action through the union by far exceeded the very old successful appeal to an industrial tribunal.

Nonetheless there was very little the union could do to invalidate widely held social attitudes formed on the notion of male superiority. Women in general continued to visualise unions as male dominated institutions with, as far as they were concerned, inappropriate functions and forms of behaviour.

In spite of the heavy emphasis on its services aimed at meeting the needs of women workers and the number of reported successes in meeting these the union was finding it very difficult to recruit women members. For a long time they remained around 13 per cent of the total membership. The irony was that the majority of those who took the step was to defend themselves and their jobs. A high proportion of their number became articulate activists. Barbara Switzer was one of these and it was her record of activity in the Manchester area that led to her becoming the first woman Divisional Organiser. In the re-organisations that followed she was appointed National Industrial Officer in 1979 and in 1983 succeeded Eric Winterbottom to the post of Deputy General Secretary.

Terry Marsland, one of many experienced women brought in by the TWU and TASS merger.

Judith Hunt who had played a prominent part in building up the union's educational services and who had in the 1980 re-organisation been re-designated Assistant Secretary resigned in July 1982. Her responsibilities were taken up by Barbara Switzer. In keeping with the policy of maintaining a high profile in the wider trade union and labour movement the union projected its leading women activists on the women's committees of the four National TUC's, the National Conference of Labour Women and on the National Joint Committees of Working Women's committees of the Scottish TUC. Marion Easedale was awarded the Gold Medal for her contribution to the trade union movement at the 1983 TUC Annual Conference.

The merger of the Tobacco Workers Union with TASS at the end of 1985 brought into the organisation a significant number of experienced women activists led by their Deputy General Secretary, Terry Marsland.

the union in print

Before it was one year old the Association was publishing. Two free copies of its magazine were circulated to every member - one to read and one to give away - hopefully to someone who it might persuade to become a member. The Draughtsman was obviously aimed at an exclusive readership but its intention was to universalise attitudes and broaden perceptions. In his "History of the AESD" Jim Mortimer quoted from the Editorial notes of the second issue. In the rather grandiloquent style of the day it said:

"It is not sufficient to have a purely parochial knowledge of conditions affecting our material welfare. A further acquaintance is desirable and one of the objects of this magazine is to give an indication of the general trend of affairs that have any bearing on us collectively or individually."

Although they may have been talking only to each other the writers, the correspondents and the readers of the Draughtsman were responsible for one of the liveliest, most discursive and in terms of subject matter one of the most wide-ranging periodicals ever to come out of the British Trade Union Movement.

Besides covering the prevalent affairs and conditions of the trade and the members' relationships with their firms (usually in contention) each month the contents of the magazine revealed the enormous variety of interests to be found among the population of drawing offices throughout the country. The contributions on technical subjects dealt with mechanical and mathematical problems that ranged from the complex to the insoluble. Political, social and economic matters were substantially analysed. On religion, gardening, foreign travel, sport, history, folk music or whatever, draughtsmen had a point of view and were more than willing to spell it out. Cartoons were a notable feature of the journal. The members seemed to have a liking for pictorial puns - a draughtsman at his board dressed in cowboy clothes "We hired him because he was quick on the draw" or cynical employers who advise new staff that "They are expected to start at the bottom and stay there."

It was the responsibility of the Editor to ensure that the columns of the Journal were open to every shade of opinion. A perusal of the correspondence pages in any issue would show how conscientiously this injunction was observed. Personal attacks on individual members were not acceptable but the frequent occurrence of the phrase "with the greatest respect" meant some member was going to say something uncomplimentary about another.

Each year the early summer edition carried a report of the debates, decisions and personalities at the Association's Annual Conference. In the autumn issues there would be accounts of the parts played by its delegates at the TUC and Labour Party Conferences.

Editorial comment which was predictably and unequivocally left of centre was in the hands of J E Mortimer who had in 1948 taken over from the first Editor C W Thomson. When Jim Mortimer resigned in 1968 the magazine was for a few months run by a committee of senior lay members until the procedures of appointing a new Editor were sorted out. Ken Gill was selected. He held the post until he became Deputy General Secretary in 1971. His successor and the last full-time official to occupy the chair was the Gloucester based Divisional Organiser, Harry Smith.

Sadly for many, inevitably for the union as a whole, the times were demanding change. September 1976 saw the last edition of the glossy and in some ways rather sedate form of the union magazine. The Draughtsman which had taken its time in becoming DATA Journal which in turn had enthusiastically switched to being called TASS Journal, ended up as the more "with it" tabloid "TASS News and Journal."

The "TASS News" bit of the title was inherited from the news sheet that since the earliest days had been a sort of companion to the magazine. It started life as the "Vacancy List" a bulletin that had two main purposes; one was to advertise jobs where the employer was willing to pay not less than the Association minimum rate, the second was to "post" firms where members were in dispute or where the union had been refused recognition. The idea was to advise members where good pay and conditions might be available and to let them know what firms to stay away from. At the end of 1962 the Vacancy List was joined by "Industrial News from DATA" which, as the title suggested, provided information and comment on the current industrial scene. The

AIMING HIGH... The fondly remembered *Draughtsman* served the union and its membership with distinction

following year the EC decided to replace the Vacancy List, Industrial News from DATA and the Branch Secretaries Parliamentary News with a single weekly newsletter simply called DATA News. Editorial responsibility was in the hands of the General Secretary until 1962. It was then passed to the Editor of the Journal.

When it was decided in 1975 that the Editor of the Journal should no longer be a full-time official of the union with an industrial as well as a journalistic role, the job went to Pat Smith, one of the most experienced members of the editorial staff.

The membership appeared to absorb the culture shock brought about by the transformation of their Journal. Out went the leisurely literary compositions and thoughtful essays. In came the compressed and concentrated rhetoric of the tabloid. TASS News and Journal was now a campaigning gazette. Its role was to arm the members with information to defend their jobs and their rights at work. Special features included race relations, the peace movement, women's rights, youth training schemes, health and safety at work, pension schemes and company information. In true tabloid fashion it challenged, it exposed and it asserted. With the amalgamations that brought the craft sectors into the union it acquired a special Craft News Supplement covering items of interest to these particular groups of members.

Pat Smith retired in 1980 and Mitch Howard assisted by an experienced staff took over as Editor. In 1983 the Journal won the Special Category prize for the best treatment of the fight against unemployment in the competition organised by the TUC and the NUJ Trade Union Journalists Section.

The union's journal in all its formats had to put up with a fair share of carping criticism - particularly from those who wrote to say they chucked it in the waste bin unread. On the other hand the union's technical publications drew nothing but praise and appreciation.

Members, employers, students and librarians conceded that these booklets were among the best written, most informative dissertations on engineering topics available. Their publication harks back to the time when members were invited to read papers on technical subjects at branch meetings. (They did not have to contend with TV in those days). Someone then suggested that these treatises ought to be printed and circulated to the wider membership. And that is how they got started. They were sold to members at a highly subsidised price - two shillings in 1958 (10p in today's money).

Management of these publications was in the hands of a highly qualified lay member technical sub-committee with the Editor acting as secretary. The subject matter arose in response to an expressed need rather than consideration of economic advantage. By the early sixties something like 100,000 copies of nearly 400 different titles were sold. In 1979 TASS updated and reprinted its all-time best-seller (59,000 copies) "Design Examples for Young Draughtsmen."

Over the next twenty years DATA, and subsequently TASS, continued to enthuse over its prestigious technical publications. Each Annual Conference received a report of the number of booklets in the process of being written along with planned additions to the list. The spread of the membership over wider areas of production was taken as a sign that there would be a need for new titles. Works on computerisation and new technology were already in the pipeline. What was not foreseen was the Tory Government's policy of de-industrialisation.

In line with its commitment to keep the membership up to date with developments in the industry the union continued to publish leaflets, pamphlets and campaign posters. In the AESD and DATA this type of material along with recruitment literature emanated from the Propaganda, Publicity and Recruitment Sub-Committee. The flow of titles showed where the committee was directing its attention: "DATA and the Engineering Technican", "A Message to the Telephone Technician", "Close the Ranks", and "DATA - Its Your Union". "Youth News", a broadsheet was published in collaboration with the newly formed National Youth Committee and furnished with material written mostly by younger members.

An all-out campaign for 100 per cent membership agreements was launched in the mid-sixties strongly backed with leaflets and a specially printed 100 per cent agreement certificate which showed that the company named made it a condition of employment for the staff in the areas covered by DATA to become members of the Association.

The sub-committee now renamed the National Recruitment and Publicity Sub-Committee continued to provide a series of leaflets and pamphlets aimed at particular groups. "The Way Forward for Professional Engineers", "Senior Staff Must Not Be Ignored", "Women Need A Good Union Too" and "Negotiating for Equality", were just some of the many titles being made available.

Specialised leaflets were also being produced for particular companies. These as well as providing the membership with company information were used to develop recruitment potential in Hawker Siddley, BAC Ferranti, GEC, ICI, Plessey etc. Arising from the Tory Government's disregard for the country's manufacturing base, TASS published a number of booklets analysing the situation in which many of the major industrial concerns were finding themselves.

One of the first of these was "British Leyland Cars - Collapse Or Growth". Others followed covering shipbuilding, aerospace, British Steel, power manufacturing and the automotive industry. These studies were very well received and the union had to deal with numerous requests for additional copies from representatives of both sides of industry.

As a union that never made bones about where it stood politically DATA and then TASS published booklets and pamphlets on many of the issues where it had a declared policy.

It was DATA's initiative that brought the white collar technican unions into conflict with the 1964 Labour Government's Incomes Policy with their joint publication of Declaration of Dissent.

auew tass news & journal
2,001,208 The fight for jobs
AN HOUR FOR THE UNEMPLOYED
Staff unions agree action on claim for 35-hour week
Getting his own back
Dowty 20% deal
New members get big rise

KEEPING IN TOUCH... The *AUEW TASS News & Journal* maintained the union's tradition of informing members through high quality publications.

Other policy statements that were projected into print included those on Heath's Industrial Relations Act, Barbara Castle's "In Place of Strife", The Common Market, Industrial Training, Equal Opportunities, Equal Pay, Defend British Engineering, Import Controls, Make It British and at the times of general elections, Vote Labour broadsheets.

head office stalwarts

Usually the public get a very one dimensional view of trade unions. They only take notice of them when they are disrupting or threatening to disrupt either production or some essential service. To those who are not involved and have nothing to do with them unions only surface to be bloody-minded. This is understandable. There is nothing newsworthy in the fact that a union and employer have negotiated a mutually acceptable agreement or to bring to public notice that such agreements are many times more common than disputes. It is significant that very often strikes which get front page treatment and draw editorial comment while they are taking place, end with scant reference to the settlement on the inside. Nor is the mass media the place to find out about non-controversial day-to-day business. And it is that kind of business that occupies a great deal of trade union time - welfare matters, health and safety, legal questions, making representations about job grading, dealing with pensions schemes, taking part in industrial advisory discussions, preparing cases for tribunals and so forth. Add to this the detailed work that had to be done in keeping the union's own administration functioning. Industrial policies would have little or no relevance if the bureaucracy was found wanting.

While the industrial relations "dramatis personae" strode the stage there were behind the scenes secretaries, accountants, clerical officers, computer operators, researchers, receptionists, telephonists and messengers making sure the scripts were ready and that the entrances and exists were on time.

The Draughtsmen's Association from its earliest days recognised the importance of employing efficient office staff - often the first contact the ordinary member had with the official organisation. At the same time the politics of trade unionism required maximum involvement of the lay members in running what was after all their organisation.

Branch Secretaries were expected to handle all the paper work not only in regard to branch meetings but also in connection with members in different firms and with Head Office. Corresponding members in the companies dealt with the collection of dues, the circulation of information as well as initiating the first steps in procedure agreements. Lay members in the firms, the branches and the regions were the gatherers, the recorders, the filers and the retrievers of material relevant to union activity in the field. Head Office co-ordinated, rationalised, systematised and programmed. With the emphasis on decentralisation office staffing levels were relatively low. In 1960 when the union membership had gone over the 60,000 mark there was a staff of 35 employed at Head Office and 16 secretaries in the divisional offices.

Like any well-established business the union

owed much of its progress to the experience and loyalty of its long-serving staff. People like Sidney Reynolds who retired in 1972 after fifty years of head officer service and the late Jack Milliken who over a period of forty years acquired an encyclopedic knowledge of branch finances and membership records. Stanley Rowe as Chief Clerk served under three general secretaries and retired in 1960 after 37 years service. His son Eric after long service with the union became Office Services Manager in the 1970s. Frank Green, who started work for the union in 1946, moved through the main administrative departments: Despatch, Records, Benefits, Accounts etc, before becoming Deputy and ultimately Office Manager when John Pederick retired in 1985. Overall Head of the Despatch Department is Ron Maloney who has been working for the union since 1947. Starting as an office junior in 1950 Bernard Smith now heads the Records Department. Perhaps one of the most demanding headquarters jobs was that of Personal Secretary to the General Secretary. For 28 years until her retirement in 1981 Estelle Marley efficiently cleared the "in-trays" of George Doughty and Ken Gill.

Never did these key members of staff and their assistants see themselves as the unsung heroes of the progress from a small craft-based association to a quarter of a million strong industrial organisation. Having grown up with the AESD, DATA and TASS they shared the general satisfaction in the achievements of each step forward. They took in their stride the enormous administrative re-organisation that followed the introduction of computerisation in 1962. Introducing centralised finance and taking on the routine work of about 300 branch secretaries led to the build up of the Head Office team so that by 1970 there were 66 employed at Richmond.

In the end, responsibility for the smooth working of the union's administration is in the hands of the General Secretary. Once the lay delegates and the Executive Committee have made their decisions, it is up to the General Secretary to see that they are put into action. So as well as being the front man in the industrial and political arena the General Secretary carries out a managerial function. The proficiency and competence in dealing with the business side of trade union organisation is a tribute to the close working relationship between each of its four General Secretaries and the Headquarters Staff.

Contrasting but appropriate would be the most accurate description of the styles of the union's general secretaries. The first two were Scots. Peter Doig was a very experienced and much travelled draughtsman, intelligent, competent with an enquiring mind (he was an authority on astronomy) and despite a crippling physical handicap he led the union for twenty-seven years bringing it national recognition and quadrupling the membership. His successor and fellow Scot was Jimmy Young, a man who lived and breathed the Draughtsmen's Association.

Affable, tolerant and a fount of common sense he was especially conscious of the value to be gained from establishing national and international trade union affiliations. The first English General Secretary was Birmingham born George Doughty who conducted his office with what could be described as avuncular authority. Through the years of dramatic change and momentous political activity his was the hand on the wheel. He brought in the growing army of engineering technicians and opened the way to what he believed was the essential complement to industrial unionism, the amalgamation with the blue collar engineers.

To Ken Gill fell the task of steering the expanding organisation through the industrial and political

TAKING IN TECHNOLOGY... New buildings have accommodated the changing needs of the union. Above, **A computer is hoisted into Onslow Hall, Richmond, making it this first union to computerise its membership records.** Right: **Park House, Tass HQ from 1986.**

rapids that at one time threatened to wreck it on the rocks of sectarianism. But dexterous changes of course led it instead to more effective and workable waters and to a wide open future.

Melksham in Wiltshire is a far cry from the industrial heartlands of Scotland and the Midlands but unlikely as it may seem it was from there via Chippenham Grammar School that Ken Gill emerged as one of the toughest characters in the harsh world of British trade unionism.

Having served the traditional draughtsman's apprenticeship he followed the equally traditional path from country town to the metropolis. In London he went from the drawing office to the estimating department to technical sales and ended up holding an executive post in a mechanical handling manufacturing company. It was the kind of progress that normally produces members of the Institute of Directors and true blue Tories.

Instead he had joined the AESD and after deep thought became a member of the Communist Party. His commitment to the Association was recognised by his fellow members and workplace colleagues. At various times he was elected to almost every job that lay members are expected to undertake. He collected subscriptions, was a member of the office committees, a branch secretary, a divisional council chairman, annual conference delegate, TUC delegate and a member of the Executive Committee.

He was selected as a Divisional Organiser in 1962 and located in Liverpool. He was given responsibility for the far flung territories of

Westmorland, Lancashire, Cheshire, North Wales and Northern Ireland. For good measure in 1965 he took on the newly constituted membership in the Republic of Ireland. It was the sort of itinerary that demanded his kind of energy and enthusiasm.

The reputation he gained was based on his realistic assessment of the collective bargaining process. "Nothing", he once said, "concentrates the mind of an employer more than the possibility of an interruption of production." He claimed that if the chips were down members who showed by their demeanour that they would be prepared to take industrial action rarely had to. He had an eye for spotting talent. Right across the country there sprang up scores of active members, many went on to national level and several became full-time officials who were Gill proteges.

Transferred from Liverpool to South London he successfully persisted with the same vigorous attitudes that had characterised his experience in the North West. He arrived in Head Office in 1968 as Editor of the Association's publications. This job gave him the opportunity of communicating to the general membership his perceptive appraisal of how national, political and economic swings affected the working class. It also allowed him to display his skill as a caricaturist - an excellent diversion from the tedium of meetings with politicians, captains of industry and sundry trade union bureaucrats. His drawings always showed his good-humoured objectivity by cleverly depicting typical expressions and stances of friends and foes alike.

Ken Gill's style was high profile. Industrial relations in the engineering industry was in his opinion no place for shrinking violets. Industrial editors and correspondents who were used to staid and ponderous utterances were intrigued by the Wiltshire burr articulating straightforward trade union logic. The colourful phrases, the telling asides, the stern glare as the hard line was punched out and the broad grin that went with the salty witticisms were grist to the media mill. While the bulk of the union membership were pleased to see their General Secretary on the box, in other quarters there were reservations about having too much of a charismatic communist who made people laugh and think.

The one label that could not be pinned to Ken Gill was "trade union bureaucrat." His disenchantment with office routine was total. Consequently, he relied heavily of the efficiency of the secretaries, the office managers and the general staff. They in turn knew the boss. He was the ideas man, the forward planner.

Their job was to work out the details. In the hectic years of the on- off amalgamation and during the complex negotiations that were taking place as the craft sector expanded to bring the organisation beyond the confines of the engineering industry the pressures on the Head Office officials and the staff were nerve racking. The sustaining force was the understanding, tolerance and the conviction that went with the long service and experience of the key personnel.

into the eighties

Members of the AESD, DATA and TASS in the process of earning their living had contributed to the advancement of technology. In return they expected to share in the advantages that would accrue from devising methods of reducing production costs and increasing productivity. They learned that employers were not philanthropists and were not prepared to concede the hoped for gains without a struggle. The draughtsmen's response was to organise. It was in a way the natural rejoinder of the technically minded, an application of Newton's third law. The force of their reaction may not always have been equal but it was at least opposite. They also learned that the more success a trade union had in achieving the aims for which it was established the more likely it was to attract criticism and hostility.

DATA and then TASS had its share of media disapprobation. Usually this took the form of pejorative reference to "tight organisation", "well drilled conferences" and not the least "left wing leadership". Criticisms that begged the question what was wrong with the organisation, policies and leadership of a tiny association of specialised workers on Clydeside that attracted in a single lifetime nearly a quarter million members throughout Britain and Ireland.

Its central policy concerned the behaviour of a trade union in a capitalist economy. Consistently DATA and TASS maintained that unions ought to be as free and independent as an institution with its members able to determine their structure and working methods within the framework of the general legislation which applies to corporative bodies. In other words freedom to pursue the full potential of their bargaining power. Because workers were dependent on employers providing the means by which they could earn their livelihood they would never be able as individuals to reciprocate the authority the employer exercised over their lives. Even acting collectively in a trade union employees through taking extreme action and withdrawing their labour merely created pressure that temporarily inhibited the management's efforts to compete in the market place. It was not equivalent to the power of employers over those whose livelihood was involved in the production processes.

Even so, the unimpaired action of trade unions was never acceptable in any capitalist system. From the Combination Acts of two centuries ago to the current crop of legislation brought in by the Tory Government the law has been used directly and indirectly to restrict, hamper and limit the effectiveness of organised workers' activity. In spite of the quite evident pragmatism of trade unions a mythology was created that turned them into powers of darkness responsible for unemployment, inflation and general economic chaos. A surprisingly convincing case was concocted to place the blame for the symptoms of the disease on the patient.

The trade union movement itself has been divided between those who sought some form of compromise with legislative restrictions such as the Labour Governments' essays in incomes policies and the Tories' interference into trade union structures and spheres of influence. Dubbed moderates and militants by the mass media these divisions represented the supplementary effects of Government intrusion into industrial relations. The policies of DATA and TASS took into consideration the fact that employers had nothing to learn when it came to moderating a union's claim and a union that collaborated with them to limit the members' expectations was taking subscriptions under false pretensions.

Even in its best years the TUC never represented more than 50 per cent of the eligible workforce. And although trade union negotiations affected more than 80 per cent of all workers' incomes there was nevertheless a constant level of scepticism about the value of belonging to one. There are historical, cultural and psychological reasons for this state of affairs. But those who assert that the coming of the microchip and computerised technology have made trade unions irrelevant may be misreading history. It was the new technology of the first industrial revolution that brought the unions into existence, not as a reaction to the technical contrivances but against the way they were used to subjugate those who were compelled to operate them. The technologies that took the textile industry out of the cottages into the factories, that developed mineral processing and revolutionised agricultural production were never intended to raise the living standards of workers. Trade unionism was not a phenomenon of a particular age. It was a response to economic conditions.

Agitated by the divisions mentioned above, faced with redundant occupations in what were once labour intensive industries and with the ideological hostility of a right wing Government trade unions have to find a way towards closer, more effective co-operation with each other. To deal with transnational companies that now dominate the manufacturing sector they need to establish meaningful ties with similar organisations in other countries. No matter how new the technology or how well some workers think they are doing everyone who is dependent on a wage or a salary is as vulnerable today as at any time in the past. In the context of contemporary conditions of employment the issues are no different or no more daunting than those that the pioneers of the movement had to deal with.

There never was a time in the history of trade unions when they were free from contention and conflict. Nor was there ever a time when they failed to recover from what looked like mortal blows. DATA and TASS have shown by their efforts to eliminate the manual and white collar divide and bring unions into line with the changing industrial scene, standing still is not an option in trade unionism.

index